T0413453

The Resurgence of Ideological Differences and Its Social Political Consequences

Case Studies of 36 Industrialized Countries

The Resurgence of Ideological Differences and Its Social Political Consequences

Case Studies of 36 Industrialized Countries

Leizhen Zang

(University of Chinese Academy of Sciences, China)

W JERSEY • LONDON • SINGAPORE • BEIJING • SHANGHAI • HONG KONG • TAIPEI • CHENNAI • TOKYO

Published by

World Scientific Publishing Co. Pte. Ltd.

5 Toh Tuck Link, Singapore 596224

USA office: 27 Warren Street, Suite 401-402, Hackensack, NJ 07601

UK office: 57 Shelton Street, Covent Garden, London WC2H 9HE

Library of Congress Cataloging-in-Publication Data
Names: Zang, Leizhen, author.
Title: The resurgence of ideological differences and its social political consequences :
case studies of 36 industrialized countries / by Leizhen Zang,
University of Chinese Academy of Sciences, China.
Description: New Jersey : World Scientific, [2018]
Identifiers: LCCN 2018035608 | ISBN 9789813272217 (hc : alk. paper)
Subjects: LCSH: Ideology--Developed countries. | Developed countries--Economic conditions. |
Developed countries--Social conditions. | World politics--21st century.
Classification: LCC HM641 .Z36 2018 | DDC 140--dc23
LC record available at https://lccn.loc.gov/2018035608

British Library Cataloguing-in-Publication Data
A catalogue record for this book is available from the British Library.

For any available supplementary material, please visit
https://www.worldscientific.com/worldscibooks/10.1142/11040#t=suppl

Desk Editors: Anthony Alexander/Lixi dong

Typeset by Stallion Press
Email: enquiries@stallionpress.com

Preface

It is shown in *The End of History* which was written by Francis Fukuyama that the liberal democracy has flourished successfully until the end of history. However, there are still various obstacles to the development of liberal democracy in countries around the world. Compared with other political ideologies, such as communism and conservatism, the liberal democracy has not got an overwhelming stage, yet.

What is hard to ignore is that with the development of our society and economy, the ideological division of political parties, however, is getting more and more serious. Even in what is known as democracies, the political party polarization is often seen in reality by different parties in order to win the election campaign. Even in democracies, the influence of ideology on political reality is not weakened, but intensified. Based on this, the author, through studying 36 countries, discusses how the ideological changes that resulted from different party turnovers or government turnovers in different periods affect the political reality.

Chapter 1 mainly advances some novel approaches to measuring the impact of party ideologies on political efficiency, which fills the gap that we are lack of effective methods to elucidate the degree of party conflicts between cabinet and parliament, even though scholars have distinguished between the unified government and the divided government. Besides, the author further measures the identity and differentiation index between political parties in control of the executive and legislative branches.

Chapter 2 analyzes the impact of political turnover on government effectiveness and economic growth, which has long been deemed to be complex and difficult to make clear. Using the methods that are referred to in the previous chapter, the author finds that the political turnover may differ in their effects on government effectiveness, depending on countries themselves. While the effect on economic growth is insignificant, to be more precise, although government turnover might result in short-term economic fluctuations in some countries, its long-term effects on economy are insignificant.

Chapter 3 studies the impact of political parties' position on the left-right ideology scale on social security policy, whose findings have added that except for the left-wing, the right-wing incumbency is also inclined to spend more on social security in some democracies. In addition, I also find that the impacts of the left–right scale on social security expenditure may differ at some certain periods of time or the levels of welfare in some particular states.

Chapter 4 mainly discusses the generally ignored relationship between workers' strikes and ideological turnover, which has arrived at a conclusion that the activity level of strikes affects ideological turnover with lags. Conversely, the ideological turnover has no significant current or lagged effect on strikes.

In the end, I would like to express my heartfelt thanks to the editors, Mr. Anthony Alexander and Miss Lixi Dong, as well as the World Scientific Publishing Company. Thank you for your kindly help and approval. In addition, I'm grateful to the senior fellows in Peking University, University of Tokyo, too many names to mention, in this field. Owing to your research, I can broaden my mind and conduct the researches in this book. Last but not least, I'd like to thank all the contributors to this book from its design to publication. Without your efforts, this book cannot come out successfully.

About the Author

Dr. Leizhen Zang is an Associate Professor at the School of Public Policy and Management, University of Chinese Academy of Sciences, China. He is also a Japan Foundation Fellow at the Institute for Advanced Studies on Asia in the University of Tokyo and a research fellow at the Institute of State Governance in Peking University. His research covers comparative politics and public policy. His articles have been published in international peer reviewed journals, such as *Research Policy, Technology Analysis & Strategic Management, Social Science Computer Review, Telecommunication Policy, China: An International Journal*, etc. He has published an English book with Springer and Chinese ones with Social Sciences Academic Press (China) and Social Sciences Press. His current projects include being a co-author for the monograph *Internet, Institution, and Innovation: Re-Interpreting the Complex Developmental Future of Our World* published by Oxford University Press and being involved in the translations of *The Oxford Handbook of Political Methodology and The Oxford Handbook of Public Policy* with Chinese People's Publishing House. He is also the applicant and lead researcher for National Social Science Foundation of China.

Contents

Preface v

About the Author vii

Chapter 1 Getting Along: Novel Approaches to Measuring the Impact of Party Ideologies on Political Efficiency 1

Chapter 2 Government Turnover, Governance Effectiveness, and Economic Growth: Evidence from 36 Industrialized Countries 25

Chapter 3 Does Ideology Matter? Political Parties and Social Security Policies in Democracies 77

Chapter 4 Strikes of Workers and Ideological Turnover in Democracies: A Panel Vector Auto-regression Approach 99

Bibliography 135

Index 153

Chapter 1

Getting Along: Novel Approaches to Measuring the Impact of Party Ideologies on Political Efficiency*

Party government has long been a focus of scholars, who have distinguished concepts of unified government and divided government (minority government) based on seat differences in government (cabinet) and parliament parties. However, such studies have been unable to obtain effective methods to elucidate the degree of party conflicts between cabinet and parliament. This chapter introduces and describes several novel measurement methods, such as Euclidean distance and Cosine distance, and compares their advantages along with disadvantages. We further measure identity and differentiation index between political parties in control of the executive and legislative branches.

1. Introduction

Since the publication of Schattschneider's *Party Government* in 1942 (Schattschneider, 1942), party government has been the focus for a wide variety of scholarly studies. It is widely understood that political parties

*I acknowledge the helpful comments and programming of Dr Weimin Jiang on this chapter.

enforce their policy proposals by controlling the government. However, the dynamics of multi-power politics frequently prevent any single party from dominating the government for extended periods of time. Therefore, the ruling party faces difficulties in implementing policies. On the one hand, the policies of ruling party may be opposed by parties out of power, and on the other hand, in coalition government consisting of multi-parties, different parties can hardly reach consensus on policies on the basis of their own interests and ideologies.

In the case of the United States, both unified government and divided government can be seen under different periods. Unified government is a type of government in which a political party is in control of the administrative system and holds more than half of the seats in the legislature (Laver & Shepsle, 1990a). In contrast to the concept of unified government, a divided government is a type of government in which the political party governing the executive branch does not own a majority of seats in Congress (Menefee-Libey, 1991). In a unicameralism regime, when the political party holding a majority of seats in Congress is not the party governing the executive branch, the government is called a divided government. In a bicameralism regime, when most seats in the lower house or the upper house are occupied by the non-ruling party, the government can be called a divided government. The governing party is the link between the executive and the legislature branches, but in a divided government, policies proposed by the executive branch can seldom receive support from the parliamentary majority. Divided governments have frequently appeared since World War II, which has drawn much scholarly attention. A study found that "between 1897 and 1954, divided parties' control of government occurred 14% of the time, between 1955 and 1990, two-thirds of the time" (Binder, 1996). At the level of local government in the US, it is increasingly common that the state governor and the state legislature leader are from different political parties, with the proportion of unified governments decreasing year by year after 1946, and approximately 75% of state governments becoming divided governments after 1988 (Fiorina, 1991). In a research report, Sundquist (1988) has pointed out that the US polity is facing a period when a divided government will be the norm.

Divided governments are common in countries with a presidential system like America or countries with a two-headed executive system such as France. In countries with a cabinet system, members of the parliament are elected by universal suffrage and the political party winning a majority of seats in parliament becomes the ruling party, with its party chieftain being appointed as prime minister or premier after the approval from the head of state and organizing cabinet. However, from time to time, none of the political parties in cabinet system can obtain a majority of seats, and at that time every party compromises to elect a premier and form a coalition cabinet. In Europe, the multi-party context that has emerged since the end of World War II has insured the presence of coalition governments. Since the 1970s, studies about the form and duration of coalition government have increased and scholars have focused more attention on analyzing different parties' seats, roles, and impacts on decision-making in coalition governments (Budge & Laver, 2016; Cheibub & Przeworski, 2004; Dodd, 2015; Laver & Shepsle, 1990b). With the exception of coalition governments, where the cabinet is formed by a political party with less than half of the available congressional seats, the government is referred to as either a minority government or a non-majority government (Shugart, 1995). Data from Israel, Canada, and 13 European countries with cabinet systems show that 125 out of 365 party alternations have led to minority governments (Strøm, 1990). Cheibub (2002) has shown that approximately one third of parliamentary nations do not organize majority coalitions but organize cabinets in the form of a minority government. In such a government, the ruling party cannot command the government and parliament simultaneously.

Regardless of differences between presidential and cabinet systems, Elgie (2001) argues that when the president, premier, and principle cabinet members belong to the same political party which does not occupy over 50% of seats in parliament, countries with cabinet systems can also form divided government in the manner of countries with presidential systems. When the president and premier belong to different parties and the premier receives support from a majority of Congressional members, the government is called a cohabitated, or split-executive government. By observing all democratic countries in the period from 1946 to 1999, Cheibub and Przeworski (2004) found that the number of ruling parties that did not own over 50% of seats in Congress within presidential or cabinet systems is far larger than commonly assumed. In countries with cabinet systems, 282 (56.8%) out of 498 investigations showed that none of any political parties can occupy a majority of seats in Congress, and in presidential countries, 97 (44.5%) out of 218 investigations indicated that the president's party cannot control more than half of the seats in Congress. Our research has further pointed out that the legislative efficiency of minority governments has not diminished compared with that of majority coalition governments.

In all countries examined, it is common that one party may control the executive branch while one or both houses of the legislative branch may be controlled by another party. But data of extant studies on this topic are mainly obtained on the basis of human labor. With the increase of leadership transitions globally, the volume of relevant potential data worth analyzing has, at present, exceeded the capacity to do so. Further complicating the collection and analysis of data is variability in the state of a majority congress. The governing party can command the executive and a majority of Congressional seats concurrently, and the number of occupied seats may be a supermajority, simple majority, or plurality. Measuring the degree of disproportionality which might occur within multi-party systems, also creates challenges for the study. Furthermore, current studies have implied a false hypothesis that disparities of ideologies among all parties do not generate effects on the current political situation. All political parties need to choose among three options: influencing government decisions, controlling the government or wining voters' support, but bargaining conditions of political parties with diversified ideologies are dissimilar (Müller & Kaare, 1999). The ideological polarization of political parties could result in severe conflicts in interest, however, its impacts on political situations have not received full attention from scholars.

This chapter examines and applies several novel methods for measuring and comparing the identity and differentiation index between political parties in control of the executive branch and those in charge of the legislative branch. The authors provide more objective methods than traditional ways to assess the impact resulting from party conflict and party polarization on government performance, leadership efficiency, and legislative productivity. Besides, our findings also offer productive insights into strategic voting behaviors.

2. Political Party Conflicts and Traditional Approaches on Measuring Ideological Differences

How to measure the degrees of different ideological political parties' controls over the government and parliament? Many scholars have measured the controls by searching for historical statistics on the distribution of congressional seats among political parties and appraising legitimate productivities. For example, through analyzing important legislative enactments in the postwar period, Coleman (1999) discovered that "a unified government produces greater quantities of significant enactments and is more responsive to the public mood than a divided government". Similarly, by analyzing legislative enactments during the period from 1947 to 1990, David Mayhew's *Divided We Govern* argued that no difference exists between legislative advantages of divided governments and those of unified governments (Mayhew, 2005).

Some scholars have measured whether the political party holding a majority of seats is the governing party by analyzing the pass rate or failure rate of governmental proposals or bills supported by the government (Cheibub, Przeworski, & Saiegh, 2002). In addition, some researchers have analyzed conflicts between the president's party and the parliament by observing whether the president exercises their available veto authority (Rohde & Simon, 1985).

Ideally, competitions among political parties would create a stable environment whereby the opposition party would supervise the party ruling both the executive and legislative branches. However, in a divided or non-majority government, the separation of the administrative and legislative power could seriously weaken the operating principles of the government and encourage conflicts between the executive and legislative branches, resulting in a loss of efficiency. Impacts of conflicts among political parties on the current political situation are illustrated in the following aspects: first, party conflicts affect governmental performance and leadership efficiency. Some studies have strongly suggested that divided governments more often end up in a policy gridlock between the administrative and legislative branches (Cutler, 1988; Leonard, 1991;

Sundquist, 1989). Linz and Valenzuela (1994) have described how a divided government could easily cause policy disputes between government and parliament while reducing efficiency in enacting government policies. The country's overall economic performance is also improved under a unified government because relevant policies might be implemented more smoothly (Alesina, Rosenthal, Calvert, & Eggertsson, 1995; Mccubbins, 1991).

Second, party conflicts bring impacts on legislation productivity (Jones, 2001; Ragusa, 2010). Different stances of the president and parliament lead to inharmonious relation between them, resulting in the government executive to lose the majority, and be unable to pass legislation at will. In countries with cabinet systems, when bills of the coalition government or the minority government fail to pass, the government has to step down. Therefore, the government is cautious in proposing policies, which results in policy lag. Some scholars hold opposite opinions. For example, Mayhew (1991) found that no obvious disparity exists between outcomes of government policies or acts of unified governments and those of divided governments by analyzing the relation between the American government and parliament after World War II. Mayhew concluded that divided governments do not necessarily lead to stalemate and gridlock in legislation, or differences in decision results. Many scholars challenge the validity of Mayhew's approach to identifying significant legislations (Clinton & Lapinski, 2006; Howell, Adler, Cameron, & Riemann, 2000). By developing alternative measures of statute significance and legislative performance, scholars have also challenged the null result of the impact from divided governments on law-making and have presented contrary findings that divided governments do impact on Congress's legislative outcomes (Kriner & Schwartz, 2008; Krutz, 2000).

Last but not least, party conflicts impact on political stabilities. Members of coalition cabinets achieve political power maximization via bargaining with different political parties. Different bargaining conditions and ideologies between parties in parliament bring about political parties' different policy preferences (Strøm, 1990). Coalition bargaining causes the incumbent government to play important roles in the allocation of cabinet portfolios in the new government and influences the independence of the new government, which results in the instabilities of coalition governments.

While contributing greatly to the field, such studies contain apparent limitations. First, scholars have ignored an essential parameter, the impacts of ideologies' similarities and differences of different parties. Political parties with similar or mutually compatible ideologies may find it easier to cooperate or maintain the stabilities of coalition governments. The greater the ideological distinctions among parties are, the less likely they are to effectively cooperate. Second, even in divided, minority or coalition governments, the possible distributions of seats among parties with different ideologies are virtually infinite, but efforts to measure subtle changes and impacts brought by the changes are limited.

3. Comparison of Different Measurement Methods

In order to achieve the goal of our research, political parties have been divided into left-wing, right-wing and center parties based on ideological differences. The percentage of seats occupied by each party in both parliament and government are then tracked for later comparisons. Finally, the methods described in this chapter use real data to analyze how the ideological differences of political parties in cabinet and parliament affect government efficiency.

There is a relatively direct method to determine if the party has a majority of seats both in parliament and in cabinet. Generally speaking, the most direct method to find out which party in cabinet and parliament takes most seats is the subtraction or division between historical data from various countries. Take the analysis between left-wing party and right-wing party for example. If their percentages are subtracted, the absolute bias will be acquired; if divided, the relative bias will be acquired.

3.1. *Subtraction*

In the case of cabinet, $bias11 = left1 - right1$ denotes the absolute bias between left-wing party and right-wing party, while $bias12 = left2 - right2$

denotes its parliament counterpart. Although bias11 and bias12 can illustrate the absolute gap between left-wing parties and right-wing parties in cabinet and parliament, it is still unclear whether the majority party in cabinet is identical with that in parliament. Therefore, bias11 is further divided by bias12, which is cons1 = bias11/bias12. If the result of cons1 is positive, then the majority parties in cabinet and parliament will be the same; if negative, then will not.

3.2. *Division*

Apart from the absolute bias among parties, their relative bias can also be measured. Still taking left-wing party and right-wing party as examples, in the case of cabinet, bias21 = left1/right1 denotes their relative bias, while bias22 = left2/right2 denotes its parliament counterpart. If bias21>1, then left-wing party will possess more seats than right-wing party in cabinet and the result will be in reverse when bias21<1. The process for parliament is the same.

By means of subtraction and division, relatively direct indicators are obtained to determine the overall proportion of each party within the legislative body. However, there are disadvantages of this method that are worth indicating. In formula cons1, for example, if the denominator is zero, then the indicator will be null. To patch this defect, the indicator is introduced to function sigmoid as x, and its result y becomes a new indicator ranging from 0 to 1. Function sigmoid (logistic form) is listed as follows:

$$y = \frac{1}{1+e^{-x}} \tag{1}$$

The above methods, however, may only be applied to a situation with two parties as adding more than two parties to the calculation would significantly complicate the process. But in reality, most cabinets and parliaments are composed of more than two parties with different ideologies. To remedy the deficiencies of earlier methods, the authors offer a new approach using three variables instead of the far more limiting two used by previous methods. Three types of parties, left, right, and center, are assigned spatial coordinates and labeled A and B, respectively. The ideological consistency between cabinet's and parliament's major parties is correlated with the proximity of A and B. Euclidean distance and Cosine distance are used in this research.

3.3. *Euclidean distance*

Euclidean distance is the straight-line distance between two points in Euclidean space. The Euclidean distance between points A and B is the length of the line segment connecting them. If $A = (A_{\text{left}}, A_{\text{center}}, A_{\text{right}})$ and $B = (B_{\text{left}}, B_{\text{center}}, B_{\text{right}})$ are two points in Euclidean 3-dimensional space, then the distance (cons3_{AB}) from A to B, or from B to A is given by the Pythagorean formula:

$$\text{cons3}_{AB} = \sqrt{(A_{\text{left}} - B_{\text{left}})^2 + (A_{\text{center}} - B_{\text{center}})^2 + (A_{\text{right}} - B_{\text{right}})^2} \tag{2}$$

where A and B represent cabinet and parliament respectively. If cons3 is zero, then the ideology of a cabinet's major party is completely identical with its parliament counterpart. The larger the cons3 is, the longer the spatial distance between the three types of parties becomes, which enlarges the ideological discrepancy between cabinet and parliament.

3.4. *Cosine distance*

Cosine distance is a measure of similarity between two non-zero vectors in positive space. If the angle between two vectors is less than 90°, the ideologies of the two majority parties will be in accordance with each other; if the angle is 180°, the ideologies will run in opposite directions. With the method of Cosine distance, A denotes the percentages of different parties in cabinet while B denotes those in parliament, whose distance is measured with $\cos(A, B)$. When $\cos(A, B) = 1$, the ideologies of controlling parties in government and parliament are of total similarity; when $\cos(A, B) = -1$, the ideologies are entirely opposite. That is to say $\cos(A, B)$ varies from -1 to 1, with the consistency of parties' ideologies in cabinet and parliament monotonically increasing. The two sets of vectors are coordinated as $A = (x_1, x_2, \ldots, x_n)$ and $B = (y_1, y_2, \ldots, y_n)$, where $(x_1, x_2, \ldots, x_n)$ represent the percentages of different parties in cabinet and $(y_1, y_2, \ldots, y_n)$ represent those in parliament. The specific formula of Cosine distance is presented as follows:

$$\text{cons4} = \cos\theta = \frac{\vec{x}\vec{y}}{\|x\|\|y\|} = \frac{x_1y_1 + x_2y_2 + \cdots + x_ny_n}{\sqrt{x_1^2 + x_2^2 + \cdots + x_n^2}\sqrt{y_1^2 + y_2^2 + \cdots + y_n^2}} \quad (3)$$

Both Euclidean distance and Cosine distance may be used to reliably determine if the majority parties in cabinet and parliament are the same, with a further advantage that Cosine distance can control the indicator within the range of [−1, 1]. However, such methods also have limitations: first, the party types cannot be confirmed by this method. For example, it may be assumed that the right-wing party is the majority party in cabinet and its parliament counterpart is another party, but whether it is left-wing or center party is not indicated. Second, Euclidean distance is so sensitive that it only makes sense when the distance equals zero, reflecting that the majority parties of cabinet and parliament are identical. Nevertheless, when the value is anything but zero, the calculation result does not distribute between +1 and −1 inclusive as Cosine distance does. Thus, it is not convenient to observe the inconsistency degree between cabinet's and parliament's major parties through Euclidean distance.

3.5. *Pearson Correlation Coefficient*

Pearson Correlation Coefficient is a measure of the linear dependence (correlation) between two variables X and Y. It has a value between +1 and −1 inclusive, where 1 represents totally positive linear correlation, 0 stands for no linear correlation, and −1 means totally negative linear correlation (Pearson, 2006). The correlation becomes increasingly significant with the increase in the coefficient's absolute value. The correlation is said to be stronger as the Pearson Correlation Coefficient approaches 1 or −1, and weaker if it approaches 0. We may see the percentages of parties in cabinet and parliament as two 3-dimensional variables and observe their linear correlation coefficients. If the value is 1, the cabinet and parliament have identical compositions; if the value is −1, the cabinet and parliament have opposite compositions. So if there is one dataset $\{x_1, x_2, \ldots, x_n\}$ containing n values which represent the seat percentages of different parties in cabinet and another dataset $\{y_1, y_2, \ldots, y_n\}$ containing n values which represent the seat percentages of different parties in parliament, then the formula for r is:

$$r = \frac{\sum_{i=1}^{n}(x_i - \bar{x})(y_i - \bar{y})}{\sqrt{\sum_{i=1}^{n}(x_i - \bar{x})^2}\sqrt{\sum_{i=1}^{n}(y_i - \bar{y})^2}} \tag{4}$$

4. Numerical Simulation

The above discussed methods are used to measure the consistency degree of cabinet and parliament in Figure 1 simulated data (Table 1). Method 1 and method 2 can directly reflect the dominance degree of the left or the right in cabinet and parliament, but cannot reflect whether the majority party of the cabinet is the same as that of the parliament. Euclidean distance can better reflect the degree of consistency between both parties (whether the majority party in cabinet is identical with that in parliament). When the value of the Euclidean distance is 0, it indicates that the majority party of parliament is consistent with that of cabinet. But if the majority parties in parliament and cabinet are not the same, the value range of Euclidean distance will not be narrow. Thus, the result cannot be recognized intuitively and needs to be further compared with other values. Because the chapter focuses on the consistency degree of the majority parties in parliament and cabinet, Euclidean distance is the best method in terms of the result. Pearson Correlation Coefficient has similar effects like Cosine and Euclidean distance, which, therefore, can be used as a supplement to previously described methods.

This chapter aims to make clear party ideological differences between parliament and cabinet. Furthermore, the effects brought about by these differences on government performance are also observed. As stated earlier, previous studies have reached different results regarding the impact of differences in cabinet and parliamentary parties on government performance, leadership efficiency, and legislative productivity. Despite the large volume of studies and data available, such studies have ignored the impact of ideological differences on government performance. The data in this study derives primarily from the Comparative Political Data Set

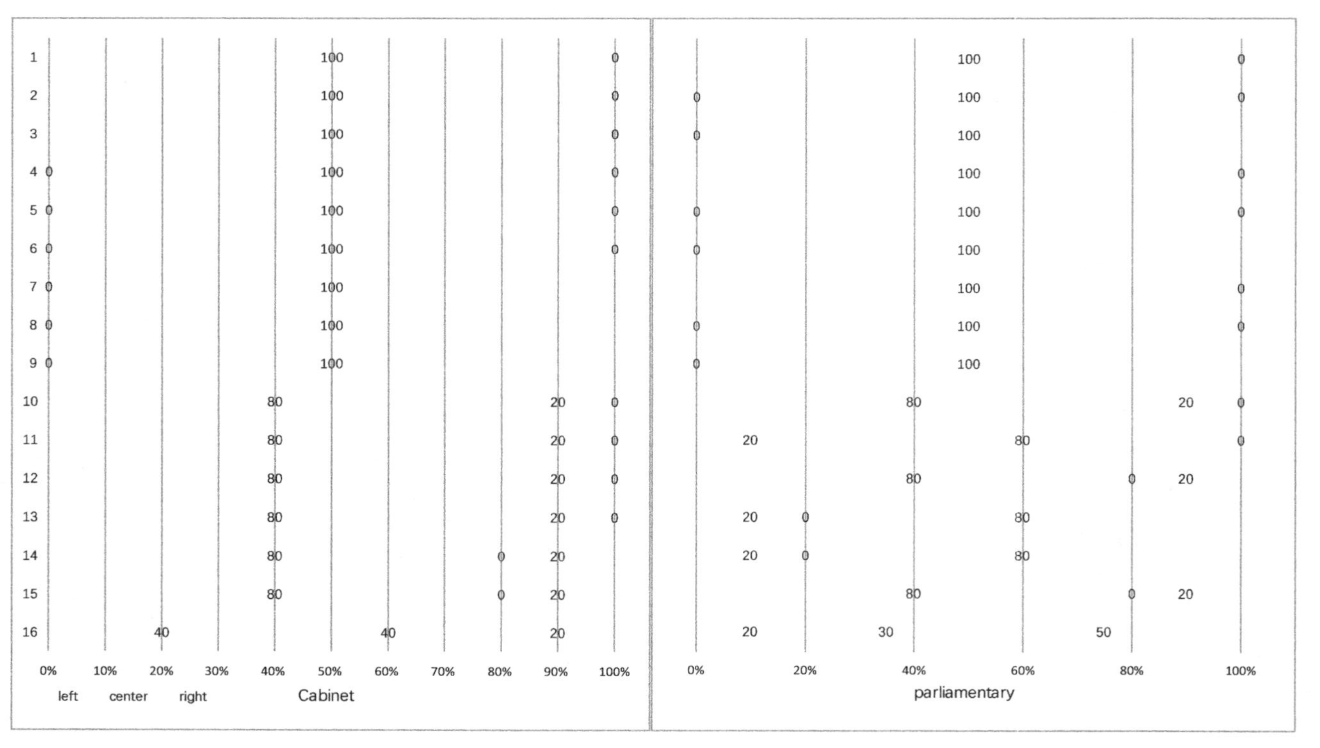

Figure 1. The seats sharing percentages of political parties both in cabinet and parliament.

Note: The data in Figure 1 are the seats sharing percentages of left-wing, right-wing and center parties both in cabinet and parliament, which are labeled left1, center1, right1, and left2, center2, right2 respectively. In Figure 1, 16 conditions are simulated, including various extreme ones.

Table 1. Results comparison of different measurement methods.

Case	Subtraction	Euclidean distance	Cosine distance	bias11	bias22	Pearson Correlation Coefficient
1	1.00	0.00	1.00	1	1	1.00
2	+∞	141.42	0.00	1	1	−0.50
3	−1.00	141.42	0.00	1	0.5	−0.50
4	0.00	141.42	0.00	1	1	−0.50
5	0/0	0.00	1.00	1	1	1.00
6	0.00	141.42	0.00	1	0.5	−0.50
7	−1.00	141.42	0.00	0.5	1	−0.50
8	−∞	141.42	0.00	0.5	1	−0.50
9	1.00	0.00	1.00	0.5	0.5	1.00
10	1.00	0.00	1.00	1	1	1.00
11	4.00	84.85	0.47	1	1	−0.04
12	1.33	28.28	0.94	1	0.98201379	0.88
13	−1.33	101.98	0.24	1	0.5621765	−0.50
14	−1.00	84.85	0.47	0.98201379	0.5621765	−0.04
15	1.00	0.00	1.00	0.98201379	0.98201379	1.00
16	−0.67	37.42	0.81	0.88079708	0.59868766	−0.94

(CPDS) (Armingeon, Isler, Knöpfel, Weisstanner, & Engler, 2016), Quality of Government (Dahlberg, Holmberg, Rothstein, Khomenko, & Svensson, 2016), World Governance Indicator and many other databases, which have been well acknowledged in the academic circle. With superior quality, the data are used in numerous studies, published on various peer reviewed journals.

Taking the sample size and time span into consideration, the authors integrate the above information into a single database containing data of 32 countries (2000–2014) to reduce the impact from missing data on this research. In this research, the dependent variable is government performance. The dependent variable Government Effectiveness captures people's perceptions towards the quality of public services, the quality of the civil service and the degree of its independence from political pressures, the quality of policy formulation and implementation, along with the credibility of the government's commitment to such policies. This variable comes from World Governance Indicator, which ranges from approximately –2.5 (weak) to 2.5 (strong). Additionally, the independent variables are constructed indicators for assessing whether the ideologies of the government and cabinet parties are consistent. To ensure the reliabilities of our research results, this chapter draws on extant research data while using level of human resources (education), level of urbanization, level of economic globalization, level of democracy, per capita GDP, and government revenue as control variables. Details for variables can be seen in Table 2 and Table 3 is a list of all the countries used in this study.

In Figure 2, it is demonstrated in the first scatter diagram that there is a kind of party polarization among different political parties in parliament, which is presented as bias1. In this situation, it will not have a significant impact on the government's effectiveness whether the left-wing political party occupies the majority of the seats in parliament, or the right wing party occupies this majority.

The distribution of left-wing and right-wing parties in the cabinet is shown in the second scatter diagram, which is expressed as bias2. Similarly, no matter which one holds most of the seats in the cabinet, the political parties cannot be seen to have any significant impacts on government efficiency.

The third scatter diagram indicates whether there is an ideological difference between the political parties that hold the majority of the seats in cabinet and the political parties that save the majority of the seats in parliament, which is stated as Incons3. If the left-wing party saves the majority of the seats in cabinet, while the right-wing party occupies the majority of the seats in parliament, it can be found that this difference could bring great negative impacts on government efficiency. In other words, the greater the ideological differences between the political parties that hold the majority of the seats in parliament and those that occupy this majority in cabinet are, the more negative effects this difference will have on government performance. Conversely, the closer their political ideologies are, the more beneficial it will be to promote government efficiency. In the following part of this chapter, we use regression analysis to further verify this conclusion.

Table 2. Data description.

Variable	Variable description	Source	Mean	Maximum	Minimum	Std. dev.
Government effectiveness	Estimate of governance performance, ranges from approximately –2.5 (weak) to 2.5 (strong)	WGI	1.341292	2.36	–0.43	0.597095
Govgap	"Ideological gap" between new and old cabinets	CPDS	0.275	1	0	0.44698
right1	Cabinet posts of right-wing parties as a percentage of total cabinet posts*	CPDS	43.60946	100	0	36.33031
cent1	Cabinet posts of center parties as a percentage of total cabinet posts*	CPDS	17.24833	100	0	26.32668
left1	Cabinet posts of social democratic and other left parties as a percentage of total cabinet posts*	CPDS	33.7686	100	0	36.29658
right2	Parliamentary seat share of right-wing parties*	CPDS	45.76875	100	0	38.62059
cent2	Parliamentary seat share of center parties*	CPDS	17.28663	100	0	26.86111
left2	Parliamentary seat share of left-wing parties*	CPDS	36.12742	100	0	38.51702
fhipolity2	Level of Democracy (Freedom House/Imputed Polity)	QOG	9.82675	10	8.5	0.314856
Wdipopurbper	Urban population (% of total)	QOG	74.1674	97.82	49.7	11.64784
Drpg	Political globalization	QOG	86.89354	98.16	43.2	11.44968
Lnunegdpc	GDP per capita (current US dollar)	QOG	4.399771	5	3.22	0.318086
Wdiinternetuse	Internet users (per 100 people)	QOG	60.02035	98.16	3.61	23.03088
Receipts	Total receipts (revenue) of general government as a percentage of GDP.	CPDS	41.45173	58.94	30.12	6.999876

Notes: 1) *Weighted by the number of days in office in a given year. 2) govgap, "Ideological gap" between new and old cabinets. The gap is calculated as the difference of the index value (gov_party) between the incoming and the outgoing governments. For an example, see the note below. 3) Bulgaria 1993/94, Italy 2012 (full technocratic governments) and first years of countries with democratic transition later than 1960. Source: Own calculations based on the variable "gov_party". 4) Government Effectiveness, in WGI database, the range of this index is only from –2.5 to 2.5, in the selected sample in this chapter, the government effectiveness is range from –0.43 to 2.36.

Table 3. Sample countries list.

Iceland	New Zealand	Hungary	Slovakia
Estonia	Denmark	Finland	Lithuania
Latvia	Belgium	Japan	Switzerland
Sweden	Ireland	United Kingdom	Poland
Cyprus	Netherlands	Greece	Norway
Australia	Canada	Austria	France
Czech Republic	Germany	Italy	Spain
USA	Romania	Slovenia	Portugal

Note: The proportion of parties of Australia, Canada, Denmark, Greece, Ireland, New Zealand, Portugal, Spain, and United Kingdom in the sample year didn't change, so in the empirical part these countries are not included.

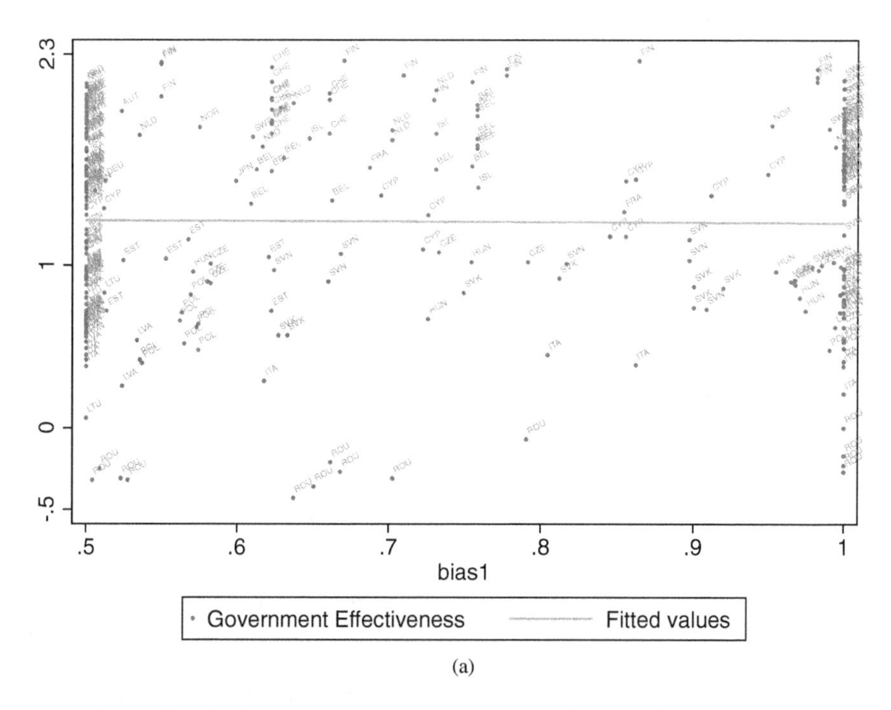

(a)

Figure 2. Scatter of government effectiveness and log Euclidean distance.

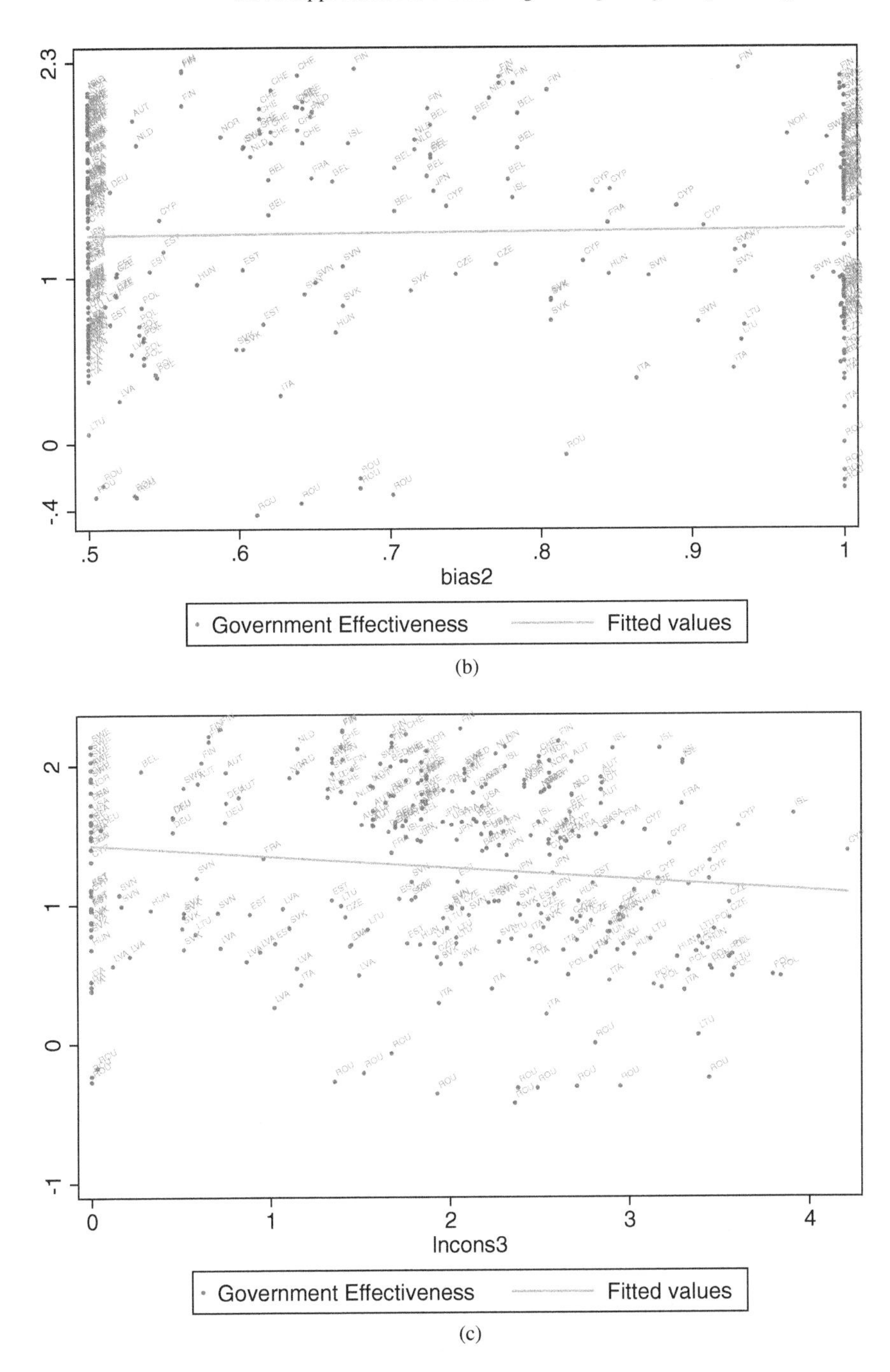

(b)

(c)

Figure 2. *(Continued)*

5. Basic Regression Result

On the basis of the above methods, this empirical study analyzes the impact that the degree of consistency of the majority parties in government and cabinet has on government efficiency. Differences in the ideologies present between political parties result in different policy preferences (Bertelli, 2006; König & Luig, 2012; Krause & Méndez, 2003). For example, with most government portfolios controlled by party A but a majority of parliament seats held by Party B, when different parties have different ideologies, decision conflicts between parliament and government are likely to occur, and parliamentary actions will be under threat of boycotts and filibusters from Party B.

Previous studies have often lacked the data and methodology to sufficiently quantify or describe the impact that differences in party ideology might have on policy changes, decision-making, and the efficient use of public resources (Budge, Ezrow, & Mcdonald, 2010). The combination of the office term and election cycle reduces the amount of change in the proportion of political parties in cabinet and parliament within one office term in most countries. Therefore, if the panel regression model is established based on this data, it would be difficult to obtain an explanatory result. Differences in the consistency degree between cabinet and parliament majority parties result in differences of government efficiencies in different countries. Therefore, the authors integrate data from different countries to ensure the operability of this research. This chapter uses control variables from studies that have illustrated how the level of democracy, the level of urbanization, political globalization, per capita GDP, Internet penetration rate, and government revenue may also substantially affect government efficacy. This chapter maintains that it is possible that the "ideological gap" between new and old cabinets could reduce government's administration efficiency. As can be seen from Table 4, except for Internet access, other control variables are all significantly correlated to government effectiveness, which is consistent with those of extant studies.

In Table 4, cons1 is the result obtained by direct comparison with the first method, cons3 represents the result of Euclidean distance, cons4 stands for the result of Cosine distance and cons5 presents the result of

Table 4. The regression result.

	Model 1	Model 2	Model 3	Model 4
"Ideological gap" between new and old cabinets	−0.102** (−2.79)	−0.107** (−3.01)	−0.115** (−3.17)	−0.119** (−3.23)
Level of democracy	0.560** (8.45)	0.640** (9.68)	0.592** (8.92)	0.587** (8.88)
Urban population	0.0151** (8.30)	0.0154** (8.62)	0.0162** (8.90)	0.0160** (8.84)
Political globalization	−0.00588** (−3.55)	−0.00547** (−3.37)	−0.00559** (−3.28)	−0.00528** (−3.17)
GDP per capita	0.335** (7.65)	0.297** (6.83)	0.319** (7.23)	0.323** (7.33)
Internet users	0.00136 (1.10)	0.000786 (0.65)	0.000866 (0.70)	0.000867 (0.71)
Total receipts (revenue) of government	0.0122** (4.52)	0.0121** (4.70)	0.0119** (4.54)	0.0119** (4.54)
cons1	0.0000115 (0.01)			
Lag cons1	0.0000416 (0.05)			
cons3		−0.00154 (−0.65)		
Lag cons3		−0.00492* (−2.00)		
cons4			0.772 (0.40)	
Lag cons4			0.204 (0.11)	
cons5				−0.107 (−0.36)
Lag cons5				−0.0658 (−0.22)
Constant	−8.756** (−15.44)	−9.116** (−16.39)	−9.934** (−5.58)	−8.801** (−13.29)
N	336	348	348	348
r2	0.765	0.766	0.757	0.757
r2a	0.758	0.760	0.750	0.750
F	117.8	123.3	116.7	116.7

Notes: *t* statistics in parentheses; * and ** denotes significance levels of 10% and 5%, respectively.

Pearson Correlation Coefficient. In the earlier-stated variables that measure consistency of government and parliament majority parties, by testing the described data the authors find that Euclidean distance is the most sensitive. Data analysis shows that ideology differences between government and parliament majority parties can exert a negative effect on government efficiency. However, this negative effect will not show up at once. Instead, the regression coefficient indicates that it is of one-period lagged. Moreover, the robustness test below further examines whether Euclidean distance is the most effective in this research.

6. Robustness Test for Novel Measurement Approach

The authors further analyze whether the results of Model 2 (Euclidean distance) in Table 4 are robust. And two approaches are applied in this Robustness test. First, due to the existence of the election cycle, no change occurs to the proportion of seats held by the majority party within a cabinet or parliament in the election cycles of some sample countries. Therefore, if these countries are removed from the econometric model,[1] Euclidean distance's significant effects on government performance can be improved. Second, in the original model, if only the results of Euclidean distance show that differences in parliament and cabinet parties have lagged effects on government efficiency, the significance degree of consistency indicators should also be improved. If these two approaches can be verified, it validates that Euclidean distance is an ideal measure method.

In Table 5, the results of Model 1 are derived from excluding countries whose party proportions in government and parliament have not been changed for a long period. Model 2 analyzes the results of impacts from lagged Euclidean distance in all sample countries. The results of Model 3 are obtained by excluding countries whose party proportions in government and parliament have not been changed for a long period and just

[1]The deleted countries: Australia, Canada, Denmark, Greece, Ireland, New Zealand, Portugal, Spain, and United Kingdom.

Table 5. Robustness test.

	Original model	Model 1	Model 2	Model 3
"Ideological gap" between new and old cabinets	−0.107**	−0.0915*	−0.109**	−0.0923*
	(−3.01)	(−2.20)	(−3.08)	(−2.24)
Level of democracy	0.640**	0.537**	0.637**	0.535**
	(9.68)	(7.40)	(9.67)	(7.45)
Urban population	0.0154**	0.0172**	0.0154**	0.0172**
	(8.62)	(8.25)	(8.65)	(8.27)
Political globalization	−0.00547**	−0.00475**	−0.00546**	−0.00475**
	(−3.37)	(−2.77)	(−3.36)	(−2.78)
GDP per capita	0.297**	0.320**	0.298**	0.320**
	(6.83)	(6.28)	(6.87)	(6.31)
Internet users	0.000786	0.0000753	0.000836	0.000108
	(0.65)	(0.05)	(0.70)	(0.07)
Total receipts (revenue) of government	0.0121**	0.0100**	0.0120**	0.0100**
	(4.70)	(3.32)	(4.69)	(3.34)
cons3	−0.00154	−0.000482		
	(−0.65)	(−0.18)		
Lag.cons3	−0.00492*	−0.00793**	−0.00611**	−0.00827**
	(−2.00)	(−2.84)	(−3.77)	(−4.04)
Constant	−9.116**	−8.384**	−9.107**	−8.375**
	(−16.39)	(−13.94)	(−16.40)	(−14.00)
N	348	252	348	252
r2	0.766	0.791	0.766	0.791
r2a	0.760	0.783	0.761	0.784
F	123.3	101.7	138.9	114.9

Notes: *t* statistics in parentheses; * and ** denotes significance levels of 10% and 5%, respectively.

analyzing the impact of lagged Euclidean distance. The above results indicate that the influences of control variables on governmental performances have not been changed greatly. All the control variables have a significant impact on governmental performances with the exception of one — access to the internet — which does not have a significant impact. In addition, from the original model to Model 3, the t value of Euclidean distance increases continually. According to previous theoretical derivations and numerical simulations, Cosine distance and Pearson Correlation Coefficient are effective methods for analyses. In empirical studies, however, these methods do not always reveal a consistent change in government and parliament parties. This study concludes that Cosine distance and Pearson Correlation Coefficient can only reflect extremely subtle fluctuations because there are few changes in party proportions in the

Table 6. Results of the consistency of cabinet and parliament majority parties in France from 2000 to 2014 (obtained by different methods).

Year	Country	Euclidean distance	Cosine distance	Pearson Correlation Coefficient
2000	France	0	1	1
2001	France	0	1	1
2002	France	13.180865	0.99208981	0.96937562
2003	France	26.010156	0.99949212	0.99953568
2004	France	6.5094163	0.99955086	0.99961572
2005	France	5.0312026	0.99908232	0.99922532
2006	France	6.9184174	0.99912855	0.99926352
2007	France	14.237335	0.99999652	0.99999701
2008	France	18.442606	0.99991484	0.99992514
2009	France	10.646131	0.99999564	0.99999623
2010	France	13.208425	0.99999156	0.99999286
2011	France	4.35	1	1
2012	France	1.62	0.99981345	0.99956421
2013	France	0	1	1
2014	France	0	1	1

cabinet and parliament of all examined countries as three separate ideological parties are examined. As an example, calculations using Euclidean distance have a high sensitivity when capturing subtle changes to the cabinet and parliament party seats for the period from 2000 to 2014, as seen from Table 6.

7. The Future Study of Structural Differences within Government and Cabinet Parties

The impact of structural differences within government and cabinet parties on overall governmental performances has drawn much scholarly attention. However, limitations of these above-mentioned study methodologies have made it difficult both to directly compare the influences of ideological differences on government efficacies, and to define the impacts of these differences on quantitative analyses. Despite of some limitations from its own, this chapter asserts that currently, the use of Euclidean distancing tools remains the best measurement method for understanding how the structural differences within the parliament and cabinet parties can influence governmental effectiveness.

By comparing and analyzing the cabinet and parliament parties' structures of 32 countries during the period from 2000 to 2014, the chapter discovers that larger disparities in seats proportions of different ideological cabinet and parliament parties have resulted in significant negative effects on government performance. Meanwhile, in government alternations, the ideology gap between old and new cabinets also brings significant negative effects on government efficiency.

The authors' preliminary explorations in this field still have limitations. In the first place, the earlier stated methods, including Euclidean distance and other research methods, did not take factions and conflicts within a party into account. Considering this, our study also extends to other new research directions such as party polarization whose effects on government performance have yet to be thoroughly described.

In the second place, if one political party does not completely control both the cabinet and the parliament, then it will become a major problem how to distribute seats between parties in cabinet and parliament to achieve optimum efficiency.

In the third place, several other things stand out in this study that we might want to note: first, the nature of ideological polarization matters, with pure divided and united governments performing better under moderate polarization, and worse under low or high polarization, with some caveats. Second, not all divided governments have the same internal political logics viz governing. Instead, pure divided governments are more capable to foster efficiency than quasi-divided governments, in some ways approximating or even surpassing united party governments. Third, the distribution of parliamentary and cabinet seats is a complex process, and the allocation of cabinet posts among political parties is also affected by numerous factors. Thus, ideology is just one of those factors. Similarly, there are also a lot of elements affecting government efficiency. So the impact of ideological differences between parliament and cabinet is only one of these elements. Therefore, further analyses should concentrate on how to explore both empirically (to address the problem of omitted variable bias) and theoretically (to distinguish the mechanisms at play) (Dewan & Hortala-Vallve, 2011; Greene & Jensen, 2016; Indridason & Kam, 2008).

Last but not least, this study is further limited by the size of the dataset as only 32 countries had relevant available data at the time of our research. To cope with this challenge, future researches ought to further test the applicabilities of described methods by absorbing data from additional countries.

Chapter 2

Government Turnover, Governance Effectiveness, and Economic Growth: Evidence from 36 Industrialized Countries*

The effects of government turnover on governance effectiveness and economic growth have long been regarded as highly complex and controversial, yet critical questions. However, existing literature remains largely inconsistent and weak, leaving much room for meaningful exploration. This chapter reappraises these relationships by focusing on 36 comparable industrialized countries between 1960 and 2014. We find that while leadership change has a positive effect on governance effectiveness, and the results remain robust under different specifications, its effect on economic growth is insignificant. The structural break points test on representative countries for explaining the economic alliances among some of these countries showed that government turnover was associated with slight economic fluctuation in the short term with the exception of Japan. Using ensemble empirical mode decomposition (EEMD), we also discover that although government turnover resulted in short-term economic fluctuation in some countries, its long-term effects on the economy were insignificant.

* I'm grateful to Weimin Jiang for helpful research assistance.

1. Research Background

We live in a world where many countries experience changes in their political structures (e.g., general election, cabinet reshuffle) almost every year. Many of these structural changes stem from the turnover of leadership and administration, and along with it, alternations in political party and dominant political ideology (Horowitz, Hoff, & Milanovic, 2009). As we know, new leaders, either by hereditary succession or by election, bring with them a different set of policy preferences, priorities and capabilities from those of their predecessors. In this light, changes in governance effectiveness[1] and economic growth, two outcomes that social scientists fervently care about, are reasonably expected as a result of government turnover.

Much of the extant scholarship has been dedicated to empirically assessing the influence of leadership turnover on economic growth. However, as Franzese (2002) pointed out, existing results are largely inconsistent and weak, and several questions remain unanswered or insufficiently answered. Furthermore, many puzzles still exist as few works to date explore the effect of government turnover on governance effectiveness. For instance, how does government turnover influence governance effectiveness and economic growth similarly or disparately? Do we observe a similar trend among countries with comparable cultures, histories, and political systems? How does the frequency of leadership turnover confound the impact of turnover on economic growth? For how long does the impact of leadership turnover exert influence over the outcomes of interest? In this chapter, we seek to revisit these questions and provide more reliable estimates with innovative approaches, such as structural breakpoints analysis and EEMD, analyzing data from 36 democratic and industrialized countries during 1960–2014.

---

[1] In defining "governance effectiveness" (GE), we follow "The Worldwide Governance Indicators", which states that GE captures "perceptions of the quality of public services, the quality of the civil service and the degree of its independence from political pressures, the quality of policy formulation and implementation, and the credibility of the government's commitment to such policies". We use data from Worldwide Governance Indicators in our analysis.

The contributions or improvements of this study over extant works are four-fold. First, this study narrows down to industrialized countries, most of which are in Europe, with comparable levels of economic growth, cultures, and democracy, and hence minimizing the effects of these factors on outcomes of interest. Second, this study systematically examines the effect of government turnover on governance effectiveness, an important but often overlooked outcome. Third, in terms of the effect of government turnover on economic growth, this study improves upon traditional panel data regression analysis by employing structural break points and EEMD analyses, where the former helps account for economic alliances among some countries in the sample and the latter delves into the duration effects of government turnover. Fourth, our findings are robust to various sensitivity tests.

The other parts of this chapter will proceed as follows. Section 2 will review relevant literature about the influence of government turnover on governance effectiveness and economic growth. Section 3 will lay out hypotheses to be tested. Section 4 will introduce data and research methods and details major results and those from robustness tests. Finally, Section 5 makes a conclusion.

2. Theoretical Development and Literature Review

2.1. *Theoretical perspectives*

What causes economic growth? From the outset, classic economic theories have regarded such factors as geography (Diamond, 1997), trade (Sachs & Warner, 1997), physical and human capital, and technological advancement as key determinants for economic development and growth. However, most of those factors "work through" institutions; that is, their impact on growth is greatly reduced or even eliminated statistically once institutions are controlled (Rodrik, Subramanian, & Trebbi, 2004). Political scientists, economists, and historians have proposed the importance of credible commitments and examined the various forms of credible commitments (e.g., security of property rights, constraints on the executive, and "adaptive informal institutions") to explain economic growth across the world.

In the institutionalist literature, economic growth is framed to hinge upon credible commitments. Keefer (2004) argued that "economic interests and institutions affect growth not simply because they influence policy but because they enable policy makers to make credible policy commitments" (p. 261). "Without credible commitments, sound monetary policy and adequate public investment are more difficult to achieve" (p. 263). Credible commitments can take many forms, the most direct of which is to refrain from expropriation (Douglass, 1981). The central institutional for this problem, at least in most democracies, is largely regarded to be checks and balances (North & Weingast, 1989; Stasavage, 2003). A main consequence of institutional checks and balances is the security of property rights, while property rights, as an institution, are important in and of themselves (Acemoglu, Johnson, & Robinson, 2002). As eloquently summarized by Acemoglu, Johnson, and Robinson (2005), "economic institutions encouraging economic growth emerge when political institutions allocate power to groups with interests in broad-based property rights enforcement, when they create effective constraints on power-holders, and when there are relatively few rents to be captured by power-holders".

2.2. *Government turnover and economic growth*

Government turnover represents a primary source of alternation in institutions that shape growth outcomes. So far, existing studies have documented mixed effects of government turnover on economic growth. On the one hand, government turnover can be a disruptive force, requiring bureaucratic adjustment to new leadership's framework and style, thus causing instability and uncertainty surrounding the issue of credible commitments (Aizenman & Marion, 1993; Baker, Bloom, Canes-Wrone, Davis, & Rodden, 2014; Feng, 2001; Geller, 1982). In this situation, uncertainty surrounding new government policy of the incoming leadership may exert some negative effects on economic growth (Alesina, Özler, Roubini, & Swagel, 1996; Elbahnasawy, Ellis, & Adom, 2016; Fosu, 2002). For risk-averse individuals, they may hold back capital and other resources and further observe the situation, leading to some attenuation in microeconomic growth (Fatás & Mihov, 2013).

On the other hand, government turnover as a result of free, fair and competitive election can promote accountability and competency — elements that are highly conducive to economic growth. While institutions matter, their effects are not deterministic because leaders can also play crucial roles in national economic growth; autocrats are usually abler to influence economic policies than democrats (Jones & Olken, 2005). In addition to the style and competency of leadership, partisanship also matters for economic policies. As detailed in Hibbs (1977, 1987), Alesina, Roubini, and Cohen (1997), policymakers from different partisanships have disparate microeconomic goals, so one can reasonably expect changes in the economy upon a shift in the partisanship of the office holder. Furthermore, political favoritism exercised via clientelistic networks can help boost growth in certain sectors of the economy (Earle & Gehlbach, 2015).

The divergent economic development directions pointed to by government turnover are further compounded by two widely documented political phenomena: lame-duck governments and political business cycles (PBCs). The sheer fact of not being electable anymore disincentives leaders to work hard; she/he may not have the ambition or will to further promote economic growth when faced with an impending exit from the current post (Johnson, 1986; Rothenberg & Sanders, 2000). Therefore, in this case, government turnover may exert a positive effect on economic growth.

Somewhat interlinked to the lame-duck government phenomenon, PBCs are also likely to influence economic growth in the short term. Since the proposal of the idea by Key (1966) and the pioneering formal model by Nordhaus (1975), numerous studies have documented the existence of PBCs in various economic and fiscal realms. Tufte (1980) offered the first empirical evidence of electoral cycles inducing changes in transfer payments, income growth, unemployment and inflation as well as qualitative anecdotes of incumbent efforts to strategically produce those cycles in capitalist democracies. Some studies focus on the effect of election year on the macroeconomy (Drazen, 2001). In the United States, after surveying the average real GDP and income growth through the presidential electoral cycle between 1949 and 2012, Achen and Bartels (2016) identified a peak in GDP growth in the third year and a peak in real income growth in the fourth year (p. 61). Furthermore, it reveals a difference between developed and developing countries: opportunistic PBCs are more common in developing countries (Brender & Drazen, 2005; Treisman & Gimpelson, 2001). By extension, government turnover is likely to have a larger impact on the economy in developing countries than in developed ones (Canes-Wrone & Park, 2012).

While PBCs may give a boost to the economy before and during election time, approaching election time can also produce negative effects on the economy, and this involves the element of uncertainty surrounding credible commitments mentioned earlier. Based on quarterly data of private fixed investment in 10 OECD countries between 1975 and 2006, Canes-Wrone, Clark, and Park (2012) documented a reverse electoral business cycle, where economic investment declines in the face of severe policy uncertainty leading up to election in developed countries. In the United States, scholars have found that political polarization and uncertainty about economic policy are potentially damaging US growth (Baker *et al.*, 2014; Bloom, 2014).

2.3. *Government turnover and governance effectiveness*

In addition to effects on economic growth, government turnover also influences governance effectiveness. To reiterate an earlier point, we follow the definition by "The Worldwide Governance Indicators", where governance effectiveness is understood to be "perceptions of the quality of public services, the quality of the civil service and the degree of its independence from political pressures, the quality of policy formulation and implementation, and the credibility of the government's commitment to such policies" (p. 4). Pietersen and Oni (2014) have shown that the alteration of government employees significantly affects the productivity, efficiency, and service delivery of the local government departments. Other research suggests that leadership change often introduces new organizational culture, dissimilar organizational arrangements, and distinct strategic objectives, which, at least in the short term, will hamper worker productivity, as necessary adjustments have to be made to accommodate new styles and priorities (Burke & Litwin, 1992; Graen, Novak, &

Sommerkamp, 1982; Tucker & Russell, 2004). Nevertheless, very few studies to this date have delved into the impact of leadership turnover on governance effectiveness.

3. Research Hypotheses Development

In this study, we base our empirical tests on a panel data of 36 middle- and upper-income countries over the time span of 1960–2014. There are two types of government turnover: leadership turnover (i.e., change in rulers) and ideological turnover (i.e., change in the rulers' ideology). Since these countries are democratic with competitive elections, we believe that leadership turnover is likely to have been accompanied with a more competent government. However, in the meantime, we remain theoretically uncertain about the effect of ideological turnover on governance effectiveness. It promotes effectiveness if the new ideology is conducive to streamlining public services and policy formulation and implementation, or it harms governance effectiveness if otherwise.

As previously mentioned, the current studies have demonstrated that various political, economic and social factors have different effects on governance effectiveness. Some scholars also have argued that party turnover caused by individual differences of leaders affects public policy preferences (Thomas, 1994). From a political point of view, researchers have mainly analyzed its impact on governance effectiveness from perspectives of political instability, civil servant turnover and demographic characteristic of officials.

Why does leader turnover matter? Because leaders do (Gandhi & Przeworski, 2007; Mesquita & Smith, 2010; Treisman, 2015). When analyzing governance effectiveness, the supreme leader of a country, be it the president, the premier or the prime minister, should be taken as an important consideration, because the incoming leader often represents different interests from those of his predecessor, which directly causes policy change and thus affects governance effectiveness. Early scholarship has attached great attention to the impact of elite turnover on public policies (Brunk & Minehart, 1984; Budge & Hofferbert, 1990; Schmidt, 1996). On the one hand, a growing literature finds that domestic leader change possibly affects international relations (Dreher & Jensen, 2009; Mcgillivray & Smith, 2004; Michaela Mattes, Ashleyleeds, & Royce Carroll, 2015). On the other hand, in recent years, scholars have been more interested in studying the impact of leadership reshuffle on international policies. For instance, Bobick and Smith (2013) pointed out that the impact of leader change on both the initiation and settlement of WTO disputes is greater in non-democratic states than in democratic states. Additionally, in a latest study, Gray and Kucik (2017) initially attempted to analyze how leaders' ideologies fundamentally shape their policy preferences, and contended that new leader with a different ideology will not invest in the policies of the previous ruling party and is likely as well to have new constituents to appease.

Despite the aforementioned achievements in current studies, there are still some unsatisfied limitations. First, early scholars have paid special attention to the impact of leadership turnover on international policies while largely ignoring the impact on domestic policies. However, policy making and implementation both at home and abroad would necessarily affect governance effectiveness in various countries. Second, extant studies have not attached sufficient importance to ideology change brought by leader turnover. Considering this, our paper takes both leader turnover and ideology change into account and thus proposes the following hypothesis:

Hypothesis 1a: Ceteris paribus, leadership turnover is positively associated with governance effectiveness.

Hypothesis 1b: Ceteris paribus, ideological turnover has an effect on governance effectiveness, which is either positive or negative.

When it comes to economic growth, it is of questionable nature that the new government has an encompassing control over the economy or that the new ideology is pro-growth, and thus we remain agnostic about the aggregate effect of government turnover — either leadership turnover or ideological turnover — on economic growth.

Londregan and Poole (1990), Roubini, Swagel, Alesina, *et al.* (1996) all argued that the possible impact of turnover on economic performance has been incorporated into cross-country empirical work about growth and investment through the inclusion of measures of political instability. Other scholars studying the economic consequences of political connections have examined the differential impact of government turnover on politically connected firms (Ferguson & Voth, 2008). Of course, there are some scholars who have claimed that government turnover can stimulate economic growth. For example, Bates and Block (2011) stated that total factor productivity growth is greater in African countries with competitive executive elections. Studying quarterly data on private fixed investment in 10 OECD countries between 1975 and 2006, we finds that reverse electoral business cycles or election-year economics exist, and as expected, heavily depending on electoral competitiveness and partisan polarization (Canes-Wrone & Park, 2012). Studies in Ukraine also show that government turnover in the context of weak institutions can have substantial distributional effects as reflected in economic productivity (Earle & Gehlbach, 2015).

Specifically, the new government may not have all-around control over the economy; new leadership may or may not promote pro-growth policies; and some may have redistribution and social welfare policies that are not directly linked to overall economic growth. Therefore, in this chapter, we consider the impact of leadership turnover on both GDP growth and real GDP per capita, and thus propose the following two hypotheses:

Hypothesis 2a: Ceteris paribus, leadership turnover has an effect on GDP growth, which is either positive or negative.

Hypothesis 2b: Ceteris paribus, leadership turnover has an effect on the growth of real GDP per capita, which is either positive or negative.

Hypothesis 3a: Ceteris paribus, ideological turnover has an effect on GDP growth, which is either positive or negative.

Hypothesis 3b: Ceteris paribus, ideological turnover has an effect on the growth of real GDP per capita, which is either positive or negative.

4. Research Design for the Effects of Government Turnover

4.1. *Data description and stylized facts*

Comparative Political Data Set (CPDS) is our core dataset. There are at least three databases that contain leader turnover information, Cross-National Time-Series Data Archive (Banks & Wilson, 2017), Change in Source of Leader Support (CHISOLS) Dataset (Mattes, Leeds, & Matsumura, 2016), and Archigos, a database on political leaders (Goemans, Gleditsch, & Chiozza, 2009). However, when compared with CPDS, these datasets only provide information about when a leader change occurs, and they do not code the direction of that change, especially the ideology of leader.

Except for CPDS (Armingeon Isler, Knöpfel, Weisstanner, & Engler, 2016), our study also collect data from Varieties of Democracy (V-dem) Project (Coppedge *et al.*, 2016), Quality of Government (QoG) Dataset (Dahlberg, Holmberg, Rothstein, Khomenko, & Svensson, 2016), World Governance Indicator and the World Bank, which are all well recognized in the academic circle and have been used in various peer reviewed journals.

CPDS incorporates data related to government turnover of 36 countries during 1960–2014 (Table 1). In an effort to match the time span of other datasets and reduce the degree of missing data, we match the above datasets to form unbalanced panel data of 36 countries from 1960 to 2011 (data of governance effectiveness is available between 1996 and 2011). Regime stability, exports, population, education, urbanization, and

Table 1. List of countries in our dataset.

Australia	Cyprus	Germany	Japan	New Zealand	Slovenia
Austria	Czech Republic	Greece	Latvia	Norway	Spain
Belgium	Denmark	Hungary	Lithuania	Poland	Sweden
Bulgaria	Estonia	Iceland	Luxembourg	Portugal	Switzerland
Canada	Finland	Ireland	Malta	Romania	United Kingdom
Croatia	France	Italy	Netherlands	Slovakia	United States

inflation rate are control variables in our analysis. Detailed descriptions of these variables are listed in Table 2.

Government turnover data are compiled from CPDS. The first variable, *leader_change*, represents the number of leader changes in government per year; leader changes reflect the result of the following seven scenarios: (1) elections, (2) voluntary resignation of the Prime Minister, (3) resignation of Prime Minister due to health reasons, (4) dissolution within the government (breakup of the coalition), (5) lack of parliamentary support, (6) intervention by the head of state, or (7) broadening of the coalition (inclusion of new parties) (Woldendorp, Keman, & Budge, 2013).

Table 2. Description of variables.

Variable	Description	Data source	Mean	Std. dev.	*N*
govt_eff	Governance effectiveness	World Governance Indicator	1.274817	0.6465799	544
gdp_growth	GDP growth	World Bank	2.488358	3.577038	1513
gdppc	Real GDP per capita	World Bank	14760.16	7131.063	1454
off_length	Length of time in office	QoG	8.43985	9.44759	1064
durability	Regime durability	QoG	49.78307	44.25068	1595
education	University students per 100,000	V-dem	39.09938	20.13595	1135
urban	Urbanization	V-dem	0.6784705	0.1391505	1658
pop	Population size	V-dem	29300000	47100000	1465
export	Exports	V-dem	68812.85	140185.8	1610
inflation	Inflation	V-dem	10.78772	62.44218	1581
revenue	Total governmental revenue	CPDS	40.58673	7.865781	1286
poli_glob	Political globalization	QoG	78.29412	17.50718	1286
econ_glob	Economic globalization	QoG	67.63216	16.45074	1286

Note: GDP is in constant 2005 USD. Real GDP per capita (contemporary local current unit) is a measurement of the total economic output of a country divided by the number of people and adjusted for inflation; it is used to measure and compare living standards among countries over time.

The second variable, *ideo_change*, means if cabinet ideological composition in the current year has changed from that in the previous year, where it takes on the value "1" if so and "0" if otherwise. Our calculations based on the Cabinet composition (Schmidt-Index): (1) hegemony of right-wing (and center) parties (gov_left1 = 0), (2) dominance of right-wing (and center) parties (0 < gov_left1 <= 33.33), (3) balance of power between left and right (33.33 < gov_left1 < 66.67), (4) dominance of social-democratic and other left parties (66.67 <= gov_left1 < 100), (5) hegemony of social-democratic and other left parties (gov_left1 = 100) (Schmidt & Beyer, 1992). This dataset encompasses the government turnovers from 1960 to 2011, excluding regime changes caused by wars and revolutions.

Then, we explore the statistical characteristics of sample countries' GDP growth rate and per capita GDP associated with government turnover. As seen in Figure 1, the sum of government changes is negatively correlated with the standard deviations of GDP growth rate and per capita GDP. Excluding Latvia, Lithuania, and Estonia, the negative correlation becomes even more significant. Since standard deviation measures the amount of variation or dispersion in a given dataset, the negative correlation suggests that the more times of government turnovers there are, the steadier the economic growth will be.

Based on the plots in Figure 1, we choose two representative countries from each of the following three groups to take a close look at the timing of government turnover and trends in economic growth at both macro (GDP) and micro (per capita GDP) levels: Japan and Italy (countries with frequent government changes), USA and UK (countries with regular and stable government turnovers), and Germany and France (countries with government turnovers that are in between the two aforementioned groups).

At first glance, Figure 2 does not suggest a clear and consistent effect that turnover has on economic growth. However, looking closely, one may find that the state of the economy is at the local maximum in years with government turnover. This is illustrated by Germany in 1980, France in 1995, England in 2007, and Japan in 2012, and it suggests that government turnover may have a negative effect on economic growth in the short term. Take Germany as an example. The economy stalled after elections

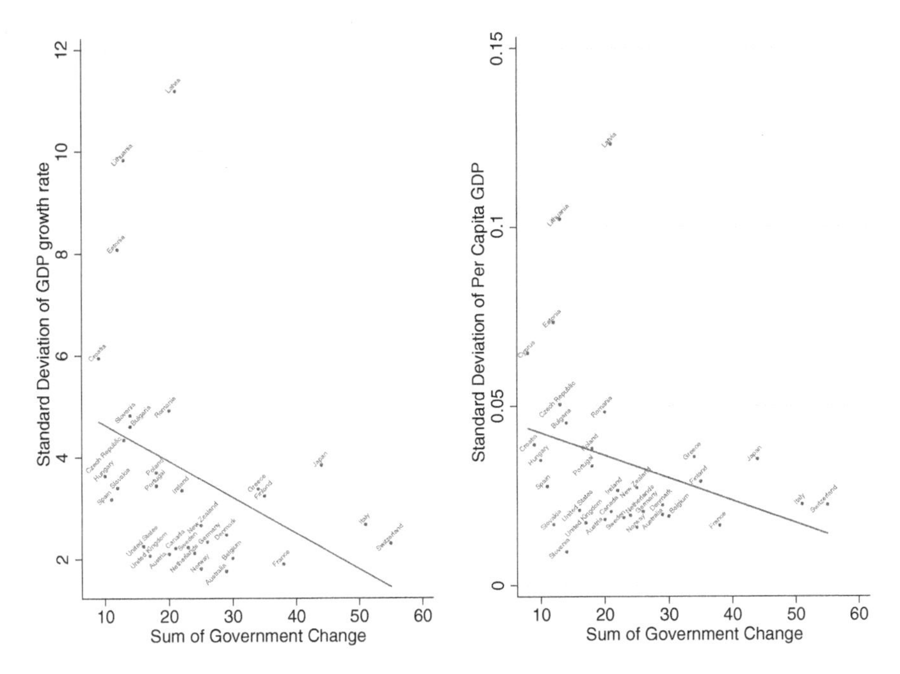

Figure 1. Scatter plots of the relationship between the sum of government changes and the standard deviations of GDP growth rate and per capita GDP.

Notes: Time coverage: GDP growth rate of 1956–2010; per capita GDP of 1957–2006; and sum of government change of 1960–2014.

in 1988 and 1998, but rebounded later, which obviously shows that economic growth may decline in years of government turnover but ascend afterwards. This also holds for elections of France in 1997 and of the United States in 1984. In the intermediate and long terms, government turnover seems to be beneficial for economic growth. Comparatively, the United States and Italy have enjoyed fairly steady growth for several decades except in 2008 amid the Global Financial Crisis of 2007–2009. This piece of empirics implies that in spite of its frequency, the effect of government turnover on economic growth is most likely short-lived.

The plots in this section indicate that the influence of government turnover on economic growth can be idiosyncratic and complex. For this reason, we systematically assess the relationship in the following sections

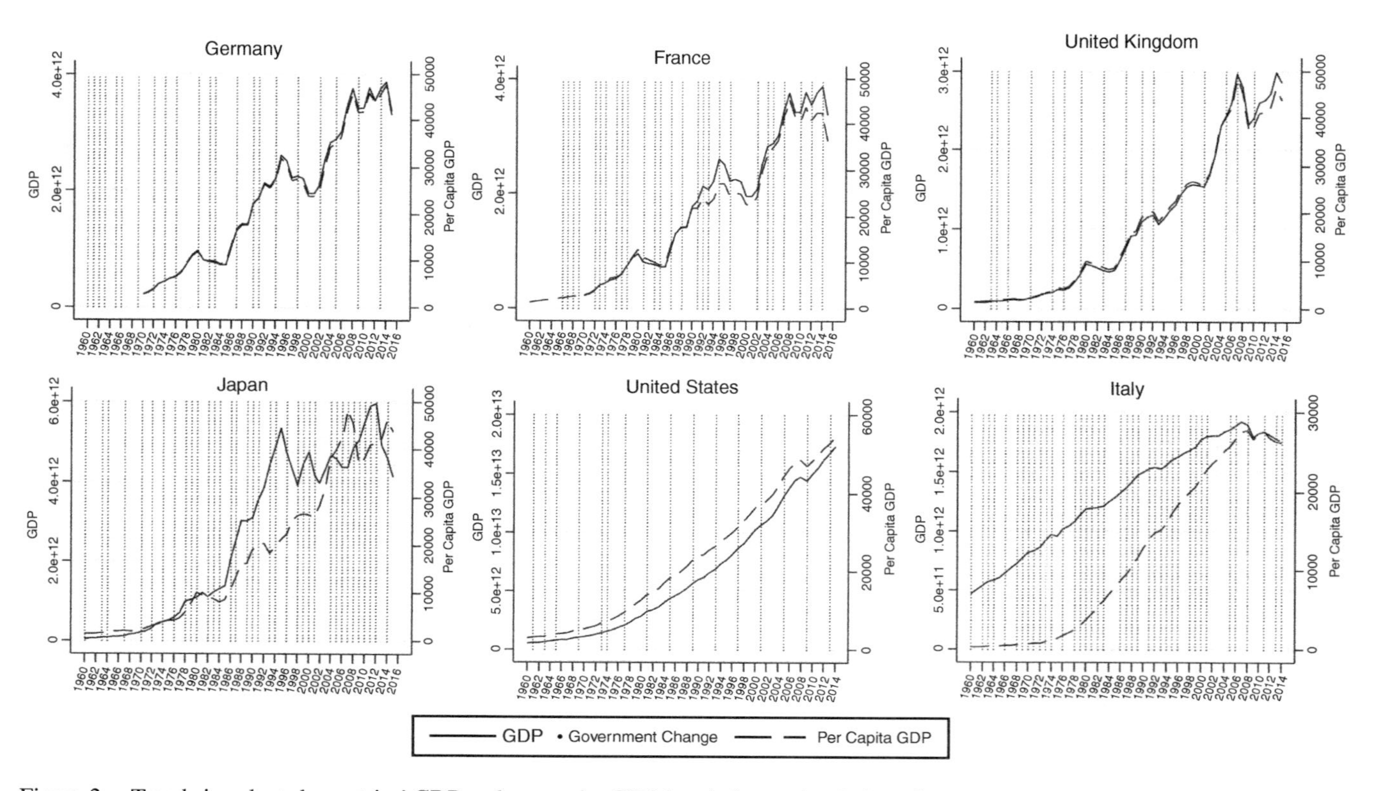

Figure 2. Trends in selected countries' GDP and per capita GDP in relation to the timing of government turnovers.

Notes: GDP is in constant 2005 USD; real GDP per capita is in contemporaneous local current unit; when *leader_change* = 2, meaning that the country holds elections twice in that year, only one point is projected in that case.

with novel methodologies: structure break points analysis and series decomposition methods.

4.2. *Econometric model*

4.2.1. *Panel data analysis*

The following econometric model is established to appraise the influence of government turnover and cabinet change on economic growth and governance effectiveness with variables in the dual trends from the data, along the dimensions of time and country-specific changes.

$$\text{govt\_eff}_{it} = \alpha + \beta \text{change}_{it} + \gamma X_i + \varepsilon_{it} \quad (1)$$

$$\text{gdp\_growth}_{it} = \alpha + \beta \text{change}_{it} + \gamma X_i + \varepsilon_{it} \quad (2)$$

$$\text{gdppc}_{it} = \alpha + \beta \text{change}_{it} + \gamma X_i + \varepsilon_{it} \quad (3)$$

The dependent variables are governance effectiveness, GDP growth, and real GDP per capita. The right-hand side explanatory variables are *change*, which is either *leader_change* or *ideo_change*. X is a vector of control variables, including total governmental revenue, political globalization, economic globalization, length of time in office, regime durability, education, urbanization, population, exports, and inflation rate. ε represents stochastic disturbance.

We conduct a Hausman test to find out whether a fixed effect model or a random effect model is the more appropriate one for different outcome variables. We choose the former to analyze the effect of government turnover on governance effectiveness and the latter to assess its effect on economic growth and real GDP per capita.

The results of regression analysis are presented in Figure 3. They show that leader turnover has a positive effect (t-statistic = 1.92) on governance effectiveness, significant at the 10% level, which corroborates Hypothesis 1a. Regime durability is also positively associated with per capita GDP (t = 13.36) at the level of 1%, suggesting that regime durability or political stability goes hand in hand with the growth of per capita GDP. As shown in the second and third plots in Figure 3, neither GDP growth nor real GDP per capita is impacted by leadership turnover in a clear-cut

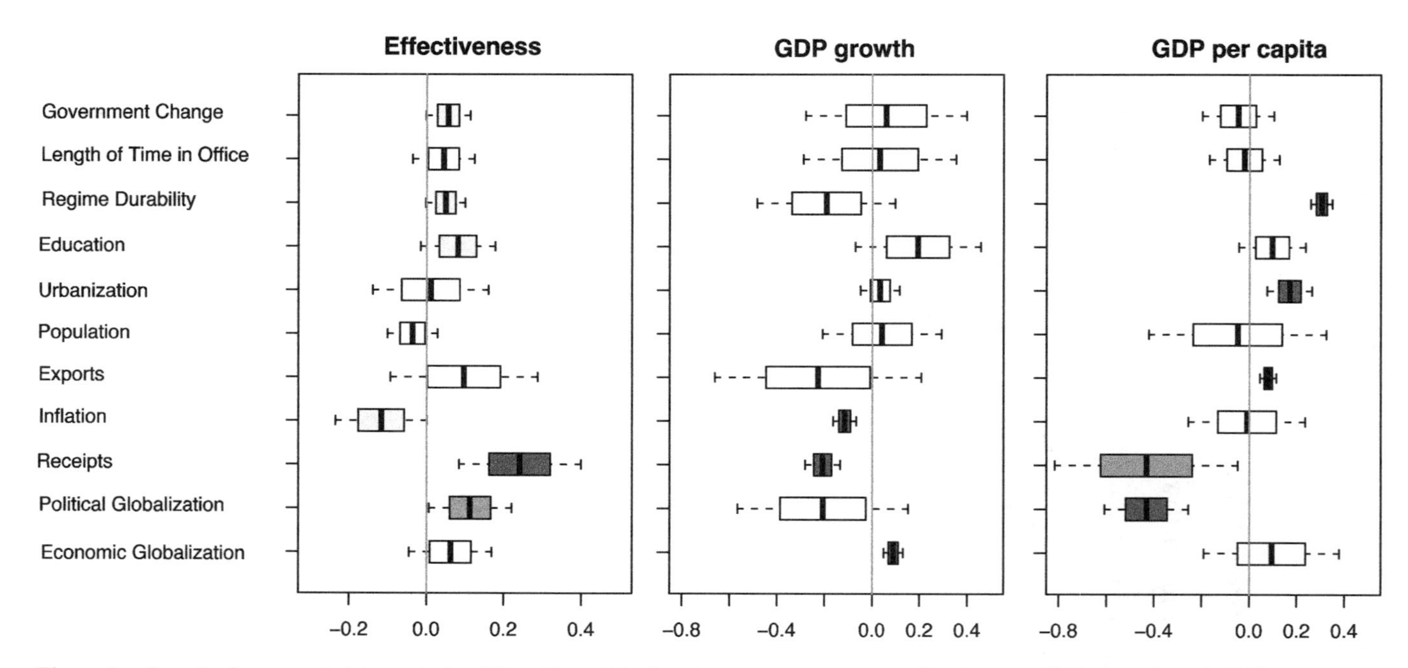

Figure 3. Results from panel data analysis of the effect of leader change on governance effectiveness, GDP growth, and GDP per capita.

Note: The significance of regression coefficient increases as gray deepens, gray (0): >10%, gray (0.25): <10%, gray (0.5): <5%, gray (0.9): <1%. Table A.1 provides raw data for reference.

way, so Hypotheses 2 and 3 are not validated. Furthermore, with the total governmental revenue as a percentage of GDP increasing, the government becomes more effective (t = 3.00) at the level of 1%. In the meantime, however, it is consistent with existing research that increasing total governmental revenue as a percentage of GDP negatively affects GDP growth and per capita GDP (Easterly & Levine, 1997; Rubinson, 1977; Tanzi & Davoodi, 1998).

The use of conventional panel data regression analysis poses numerous concerns. As we know, conventional OLS only provides the average change in the outcome as a result of one unit of change in an independent variable, which prevents researchers from being precise about a specific condition. In addition, panel regression models have the following shortcomings: time deviation of sample data collection (Bailar, 1989), measurement errors (Kalton, Kasprzyk, & McMillen, 1989), and selection bias (Heckman, 1990; Wooldridge, 1995). In the specific dataset of this chapter, we face an additional challenge posed by economic alliances among some countries. Given the fact that the Group of Seven (G7) is among the 36 countries in the sample, we face the possibility of unsteady spatial structure of variables in our model.[2] The danger of not accounting for the change in spatial structure in time series is that the model's fit is jeopardized and might be erroneous, resulting in spurious regressions (Fingleton, 1999). To further test Hypotheses 2 and 3, other research methods will be introduced.

4.2.2. *Robustness check on panel data analysis*

Robustness test, first put forward by G.E.P. Box in 1953, is widely used to examine the degree of influence that outliers impose on data distribution, the sensitivity of results due to model selection, and among others (Box, 1953). The lower the degree of influence imposed by outliers, the higher the robustness.

[2]G7 is an informal bloc of industrialized democracies that include Canada, France, Germany, Italy, Japan, the United Kingdom, and the United States. They meet annually to discuss and make collective decisions on critical economic, security, energy, and other issues that pertain to them.

4.2.2.1. Test 1: Changing sample size

We conduct our first robustness test by omitting some countries from our sample to see if the results are still significant. We order all countries in the sample alphabetically and number them accordingly. For countries that are ordered the 30th or more in the list (i.e., Slovenia, Spain, Sweden, Switzerland, United Kingdom, United States, and Slovakia), we exclude them from the subsample. The results presented in Figure 4 show that the magnitude and significance of key explanatory variables, such as *leader_change*, remain fairly steady.

4.2.2.2. Test 2: Considering an additional explanatory variable

In the second robustness check, we want to include the variable, *ideo_change*, which indicates the change in ideology of the leadership. The goal is to see how the influence of leadership turnover changes as a result of such inclusion. As the results in Figure 5 demonstrate, the effect of *leader_change* remains largely unchanged. The results also suggest that *ideo_change* is negatively correlated with GDP growth, meaning that the change in ideology — as opposed to leader change — has a plausible negative effect on GDP growth.

4.2.2.3. Test 3: Explaining governance effectiveness

In this set of tests, we want to know if the effect of leader change on governance effectiveness changes when the other two dependent variables, GDP growth (middle) and per capita GDP (right), are considered. According to the results presented in Figure 6, the effect of GDP growth rate on governance effectiveness is insignificant, while per capita GDP has a significantly positive effect on governance effectiveness. However, the magnitude and significance of the key explanatory variable, *leader change*, does not alter much. In fact, when GDP growth is included in the regression, the statistical significance of *leader change* increases to 5%.

As we know, elections bear idiosyncrasies within the same country and probably more so across countries. However, panel data analysis has inherent limitations in terms of fully internalizing these

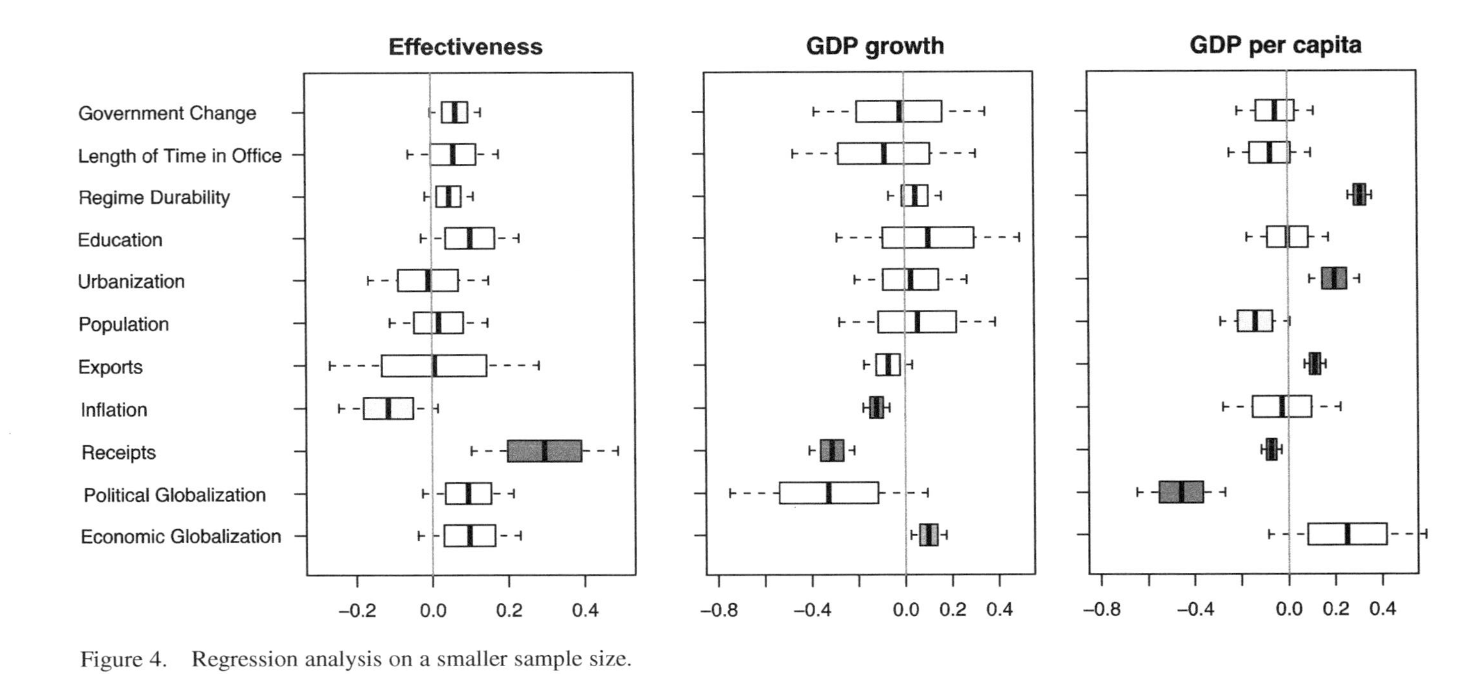

Figure 4. Regression analysis on a smaller sample size.

Note: The significance of regression coefficient increases as gray deepens, gray (0): >10%, gray (0.25): <10%, gray (0.5): <5%, gray (0.9): <1%. Table A.2 provides raw data for reference.

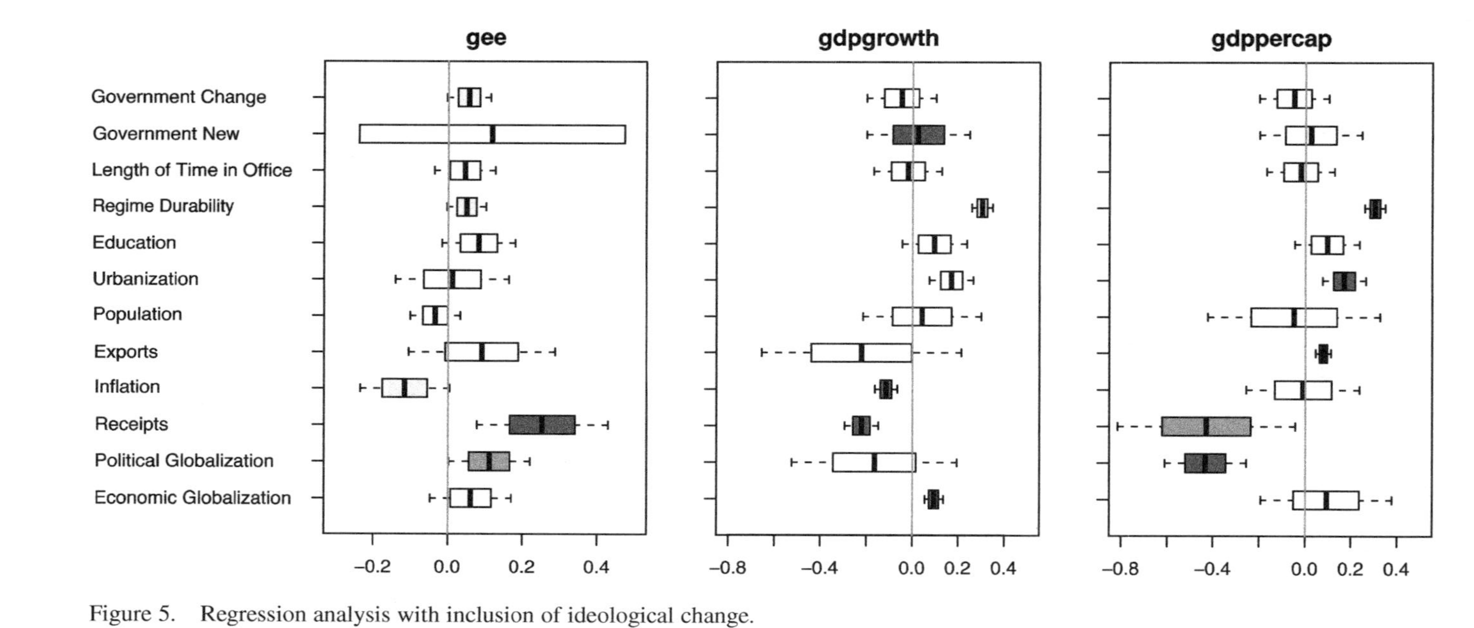

Figure 5. Regression analysis with inclusion of ideological change.

Note: The significance of regression coefficient increases as gray deepens, gray (0): >10%, gray (0.25): <10%, gray (0.5): <5%, gray (0.9): <1%. Table A.3 provides raw data for reference.

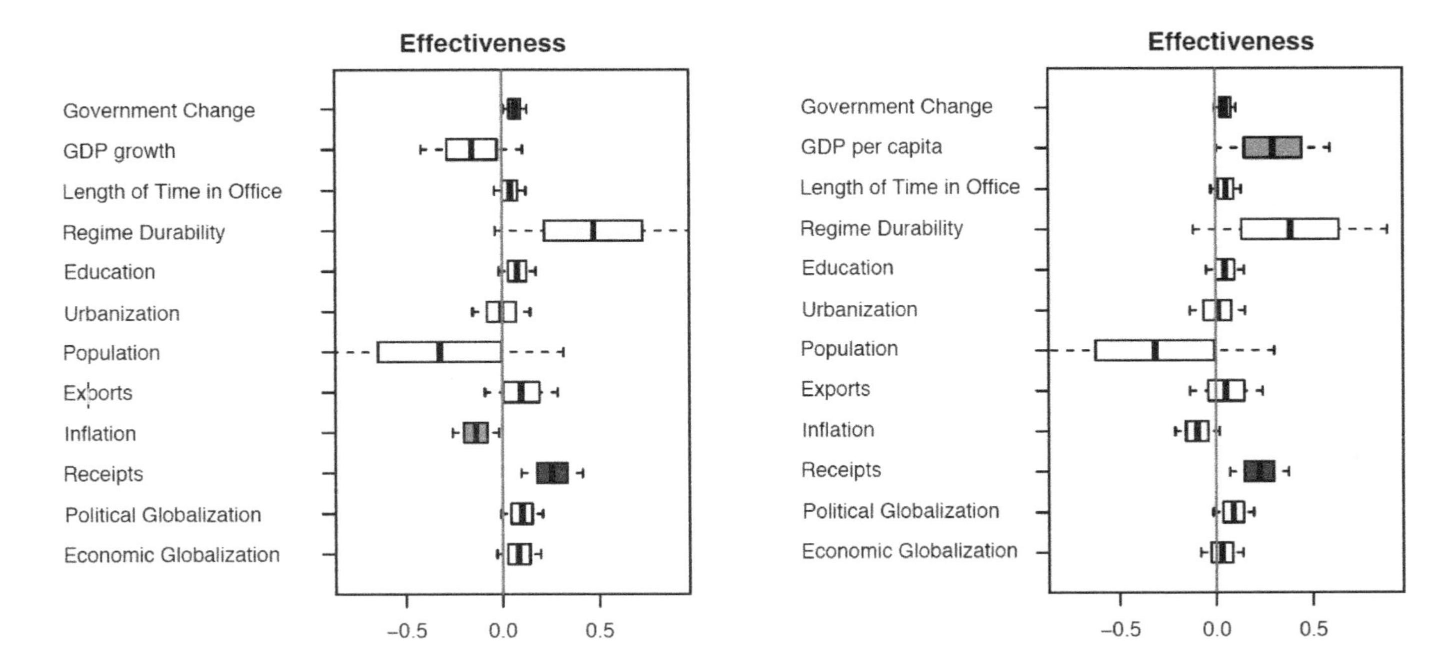

Figure 6. Explaining governance effectiveness with additional variables: GDP growth and per capita GDP.

Note: The significance of regression coefficient increases as gray deepens, gray (0): >10%, gray (0.25): <10%, gray (0.5): <5%, gray (0.9): <1%. Table A.4 provides raw data for reference.

idiosyncrasies. This is especially true when it comes to appraising the complex relationship between leadership change and the economy. Economic fluctuations constitute a time series issue, so panel data analysis is inadequate to capture this time dimension. Therefore, Sections 4.2.3 and 4.2.4 choose to focus on six representative countries, France, Germany, Italy, Japan, the United Kingdom and the United States, to explore patterns across time in terms of the frequency of leadership turnover. In Section 4.2.3, we employ structural break points analysis to explore whether leadership change is within the vicinity of economic fluctuations represented by break points. Section 4.2.4 employs EEMD to decompose the series of economic fluctuations; regresses on leadership change dummy variable using the decomposed series; and explores whether leadership change has latent effects on economic fluctuations in the short, medium, and long terms.

4.2.3. *Structural break points analysis*

The instability of and structural change in regression parameter in time series data pose many challenges, as the parameter is inherently different at various time points. To remedy this problem, we employ structural break points analysis, where we can examine the effect of government turnover on outcomes of concern within each period between break points.

We can determine break points exogenously or endogenously. In the former case where break points are identified exogenously, the Chow test (Chow, 1960) is used for years of government turnover to determine whether the economic growth series experience structural changes in years with turnovers. In the latter case where break points are identified endogenously, tests from Clemente, Montanes, and Reyes (1998) and Bai and Perron (1998, 2003) are applied to find breakpoint years endogenously. Those breakpoint years are then compared with actual government turnovers years to determine whether there is a good fit overall. Since the interval between government turnovers is usually very short and there are many government turnover years, the Chow test cannot be carried out in practice. For this reason, we employ the tests from Clemente *et al.* (1998) and Bai and Perron (1998, 2003) to decide the breakpoints for economic growth series, and then compare them with government turnover years.

4.2.3.1. Identifying structural break points

First, we apply the test put forward by Clemente *et al.* (1998) to identify two structural break points for time series data of per capita GDP. Based on the results, we identify the influence of government turnover and other political events on fluctuations in per capita GDP across time. The null and alternative hypotheses are listed as follows:

Hypothesis 0: $y_t = \alpha + \beta_1 y_{t-1} + \beta_2 DTB_{1t} + \beta_3 DTB_{2t} + \varepsilon_t$ (4)

Hypothesis 1: $y_t = \alpha + \beta_1 DU_{1t} + \beta_2 DTB_{2t} + \varepsilon_t$ (5)

where DTB_{it} is a pulse variable that takes on the value "1" if $t = TB_i + 1$ ($i = 1, 2$) and "0" if otherwise. DU_{it} equals "1" if $t > TB_i$ (i = 1, 2) and "0" otherwise. TB_1 and TB_2 are the time periods when the mean is being modified. For the purpose of simplicity, we assume that $TB_i = \lambda_i T$ (i = 1, 2) with $0 < \lambda_i < 1$ and $\lambda_2 > \lambda_1$.

If the two-breakpoint case is caused by the outlier, we can test the unit root hypothesis by first estimating the following model:

$$y_t = \alpha + \beta_1 y_{t-1} + \beta_2 DTB_{1t} + \beta_3 DTB_{2t} + \beta_4 DU_{1t} + \beta_5 DU_{2t} + \sum_{i=1}^{k} c_i \Delta y_{t-i} + \varepsilon_t \quad (6)$$

Second, besides the double breakpoints test, we also carry out multiple breakpoints test because we do not know whether the structure of the time series has changed, and if so, how many times that happened. To solve these puzzles, we follow the estimation method in Bai and Perron (1998, 2003). The number of structural breakpoints is *m*. The equation is listed as follows:

$$y_t = x_t'\beta + z_t'\delta_1 + u_t,\ t = 1,\ldots, T_1 \quad (7)$$

$$y_t = x_t'\beta + z_t'\delta_2 + u_t,\ t = T_1 + 1,\ldots, T_2 \quad (8)$$

$$y_t = x_t'\beta + z_t'\delta_{m+1} + u_t,\ t = T_m + 1,\ldots, T \quad (9)$$

where y_t is the dependent variable at the time of t; ($p * 1$) and $Z_t(q * 1)$ are covariance matrix; β and δ_j are the corresponding coefficient vectors; u_t is the random disturbance term; and $(T_1, T_2, \ldots, T_m)$ is a set of structural breakpoint years. Finally, Schwarz Criterion and LWZ Criteria are used to determine the optimal number of break points and their corresponding times.

4.2.3.2. Results of structural breakpoints analysis for the six representative countries

In this section, we focus the structural breakpoint analysis on the six representative countries discussed earlier. According to the unit root test, which allows the structural change at two time points (Clemente *et al.*, 1998), we apply binary structural breaks on the time series data of GDP growth and per capita GDP. Our results show that the break points for the GDP growth rate series are identical to those for per capita GDP series.

In addition to the Clemente–Montañes–Reyes unit root test, which assumes the existence of two structural breakpoints on the GDP growth rate and real GDP per capita series, we also implement multiple structural breakpoints test. The results can be found in the appendix. Based on the results, we select those break points whose time difference is within the same year. The results suggest that most countries do not hold government elections when their countries' economies go through structural changes, with the only exception of Japan.[3] Overall, our structural breakpoint tests do not corroborate Hypotheses 2 and 3.

4.2.3.3. EEMD series decomposition

The panel data analysis carried out initially does not differentiate short- versus long-term effects that government turnover has on GDP growth or real GDP per capita. The same drawback applies to structural breakpoints analysis. To delve into such potential difference, in this section we want to decompose economic data series using EEMD.[4] Somewhat analogous

---

[3]That is also somewhat unavoidable, given how frequent elections happen in Japan.

[4]In 1998, Wu and Huang (2009) put forward a new time-frequency analysis method, where signals are processed by nonlinear adaptive decomposition, known as "Empirical Mode Decomposition" (EMD). In this process, complex signals are sorted into several Intrinsic Mode Functions (IMFs). Then each IMF goes through Hilbert transform so as to show the

to the signal processing method in communication, economic data series are assumed to represent signals that bear varied characteristics (e.g., frequencies, amplitudes, sound trends, and white noise). We implement EEMD to identify sub-series of data to appraise the potential influence of government turnover on economic fluctuations in both short and long terms.

The specific steps of EEMD are: (1) feed data to the white noise series with given amplitude; (2) decompose data with added white noise and EMD; (3) repeat the first two steps and add new white noise series with identical amplitude to produce different IMFs; and (4) obtain the mean of corresponding IMFs of the decompositions. In the end, IMFs of objective standard are obtained (Wang, Chen, Qiao, Wu, & Huang, 2010).

Based on the results obtained by using data of the six representative countries, at least one sub-series decomposed from GDP growth and real GDP per capita is obviously associated with government turnover, with the exception of the United States, and the correlation is more significant in the medium–high frequency series. Given the reverse relationship between frequency and fluctuation, we know that government turnover is likely to have an effect on the economy in the short (1 year) and medium terms (from 2 to 3 years). In addition, the R-squared value approximates to 1, meaning that the identified explanatory variables are able to explain a very significant amount of variation in the outcome.

5. Discussion and Conclusion

This chapter reappraises the classic and complex question on the relationship between government turnover and important outcomes — governance effectiveness and economic growth, with advanced methodologies that tackle some of the long-standing modeling challenges. In terms of sample composition, we narrow down to industrialized countries, most of which

---

time-frequency distribution of the signal. However, EMD method does not adequately mitigate the end effect, so EEMD was subsequently developed to more efficiently address the problem of scale mixtures. Eventually, decomposed IMFs maintain unique physical properties.

are in Europe, with comparable levels of economic growth, cultures, and democracy, and hence minimizing the effects of these factors on outcomes of interest. We find that leadership turnover has a positive effect on governance effectiveness. With new policies and strong will, new leaders on average tend to boost the efficiency of the bureaucracy. In the meantime, however, the effect of leadership change on economic growth, measured by either economic growth or per capita GDP, is insignificant. In addition, government turnover influences economic growth only in the short term. Fukuyama claims that the history has ended in the 21st century, supposing that a particular political system may be developed to reduce the ideological conflict between countries (Fukuyama, 2006). However, we have not seen any signs of the end of the history in recent decades. The ideology divide and its influences still exist within and between countries (Kagan, 2009). Our findings confirm that the ideology does not end in domestic politics. The results remain robust to various sensitivity tests.

We recognize that there are limitations posed by our current dataset, which leave room for meaningful, future academic inquiry. The first limitation concerns the measurement of variables. For instance, as the data of *leader change* come from the CPDS database, it does not differentiate between full and partial (e.g., change in a cabinet secretary) turnovers. As we know, changing the deck chairs is different from changing ships. Future research can create and use alternative measures where full turnovers are counted “1” and partial turnovers are fractions, determined by the proportion of shuffled cabinet. The second limitation is posed by model specification, which is a subsequent problem resulted from the frequency of data points. The time span of the dataset is fairly short and election time is gauged in terms of year not month. More granular election and economic data might provide more specifications and insights into the core puzzles. The advanced statistical methodologies we innovatively apply in this chapter work better on more granular data, too. Future research can follow our leads but gather and use more granular data. Nevertheless, the carefully thought choice of sampled countries and advanced methodological approaches in this chapter enlightens our understanding of the important issues regarding the effect of government turnover on both the bureaucracy and the economy within or between countries.

Appendix A

Table A.1. The panel data analysis result of government turnover's influence on governance effectiveness and economic fluctuations.

	Governance effectiveness	GDP growth	Real GDP per capita
Number of changes in government per year	0.0562*	0.0586	–47.01
	(1.92)	(0.34)	(–0.62)
Party of chief executive length of time in office	0.00441	0.00319	–2.107
	(1.08)	(0.20)	(–0.28)
Regime durability	0.00493*	–0.0193	303.8***
	(1.87)	(–1.30)	(13.36)
University students	0.00812*	0.0192	9.610
	(1.64)	(1.43)	(1.34)
Urbanization	0.108	3.341	16992.3***
	(0.14)	(0.79)	(3.53)
Population size	–3.61e–09	4.18e–09	0.00000487
	(–1.10)	(0.33)	(–0.26)
Exports	0.000000970	–0.00000227	0.00789***
	(1.00)	(–1.02)	(4.61)
Inflation	–0.0117*	–0.0116***	–0.0929
	(–1.94)	(–4.65)	(–0.07)
Governmental revenue	0.0241***	–0.208***	–43.19**
	(3.00)	(–5.56)	(–2.21)
Political globalization	0.0113**	–0.0206	–43.16***
	(2.08)	(–1.13)	(–4.81)
Economic globalization	0.00622	0.0901***	9.421
	(1.14)	(4.35)	(0.65)
Constant	–1.859**	4.642	–7373.9**
	(–2.44)	(1.46)	(–2.29)
Hausman test (χ^2-statistic)	11.22	14.73	135.77
Hausman test (p-value)	0.2612	0.0986	0.00
Model selection	Random effect	Random effect	Fixed effect
N	47	435	435
R^2			0.888
Adjusted R^2			0.878
F			287.7

Notes: t-statistics in parentheses; *, **, and *** denotes significance levels of 10%, 5%, and 1%, respectively.

Table A.2. Robustness test (1).

	Governance effectiveness	GDP growth	Real GDP per capita
Number of changes in government per year	0.0637*	−0.0192	−51.45
	(1.88)	(−0.10)	(−0.62)
Party of chief executive length of time in office	0.00578	−0.00854	−7.426
	(0.95)	(−0.43)	(−0.84)
Regime durability	0.00461	0.0449	309.0***
	(1.42)	(0.78)	(12.01)
University students	0.0101	0.0101	−0.0203
	(1.54)	(0.51)	(−0.00)
Urbanization	−0.0949	2.518	19826.6***
	(−0.12)	(0.21)	(3.65)
Population size	1.77e−09	5.30e−08	−0.000140*
	(0.27)	(0.31)	(−1.86)
Exports	5.60e−08	−0.00000730	0.0114***
	(0.04)	(−1.41)	(4.96)
Inflation	−0.0116*	−0.0124***	−0.274
	(−1.74)	(−4.31)	(−0.21)
Governmental revenue	0.0295***	−0.314***	−72.78***
	(3.00)	(−6.40)	(−3.33)
Political globalization	0.00938	−0.0328	−45.87***
	(1.54)	(−1.53)	(−4.79)
Economic globalization	0.00971	0.0986**	25.02
	(1.42)	(2.57)	(1.46)
Constant	−2.168**	6.789	−2275.5
	(−2.55)	(0.84)	(−0.63)
Hausman test (χ^2-statistic)	9.94	20.46	165.62
Hausman test (p-value)	0.36	0.0153	0.00
Model selection	Random effect	Fixed effect	Fixed effect
N	41	363	363
R^2		0.170	0.881
Adjusted R^2		0.0864	0.869
F		6.111	222.0

Notes: t-statistics in parentheses; *, **, and *** denotes significance levels of 10%, 5%, and 1%, respectively.

Table A.3. Robustness test (2).

	Governance effectiveness	GDP growth	Real GDP per capita
Number of changes in government per year	0.0554*	0.110	−48.86
	(1.86)	(0.64)	(−0.64)
New ideological composition of cabinet	0.0117	−0.706***	24.47
	(0.32)	(−2.78)	(0.22)
Party of chief executive length of time in office	0.00448	−0.0000732	−2.024
	(1.08)	(−0.00)	(−0.27)
Regime durability	0.00493*	−0.0215	304.0***
	(1.84)	(−1.40)	(13.34)
University students	0.00825	0.0178	9.609
	(1.64)	(1.32)	(1.34)
Urbanization	0.117	3.377	17035.7***
	(0.15)	(0.78)	(3.53)
Population size	−3.40e−09	4.22e−09	−0.00000482
	(−1.00)	(0.32)	(−0.25)
Exports	0.000000909	−0.00000221	0.00788***
	(0.91)	(−1.00)	(4.59)
Inflation	−0.0115*	−0.0115***	−0.0905
	(−1.89)	(−4.63)	(−0.07)
Governmental revenue	0.0253***	−0.221***	−42.89**
	(2.83)	(−5.88)	(−2.19)
Political globalization	0.0111**	−0.0164	−43.31***
	(1.99)	(−0.90)	(−4.81)
Economic globalization	0.00614	0.0945***	9.230
	(1.11)	(4.54)	(0.64)
Constant	−1.901**	4.896	−7409.3**
	(−2.43)	(1.51)	(−2.30)
Hausman test (χ^2-statistic)	11.07	13.9	137.48
Hausman test (p-value)	0.3522	0.1258	0.00
Model selection	Random effect	Random effect	Fixed effect
N	47	435	435
R^2			0.888
Adjusted R^2			0.878
F			263.1

Notes: t-statistics in parentheses; *, **, and *** denotes significance levels of 10%, 5% and 1%, respectively.

Table A.4. Robustness test (3).

	Governance effectiveness	GDP growth	Real GDP per capita
Number of changes in government per year	0.0562*	0.0691**	0.0513*
	(1.92)	(2.20)	(1.79)
Party of chief executive length of time in office	0.00441	0.00419	0.00524
	(1.08)	(1.02)	(1.31)
Regime durability	0.00493*	0.00474*	0.00386
	(1.87)	(1.82)	(1.51)
University students	0.00812*	0.00781	0.00469
	(1.64)	(1.60)	(0.94)
Urbanization	0.108	−0.0441	0.0877
	(0.14)	(−0.06)	(0.12)
Population size	−3.61e−09	−3.24e−09	−3.16e−09
	(−1.10)	(−0.99)	(−1.01)
Exports	0.000000970	0.000000964	0.000000515
	(1.00)	(1.00)	(0.54)
Inflation	−0.0117*	−0.0139**	−0.00975*
	(−1.94)	(−2.23)	(−1.66)
Governmental revenue	0.0241***	0.0256***	0.0223***
	(3.00)	(3.17)	(2.87)
Political globalization	0.0113**	0.0100*	0.00885*
	(2.08)	(1.82)	(1.66)
Economic globalization	0.00622	0.00843	0.00281
	(1.14)	(1.46)	(0.51)
GDP Growth ~s		−0.0156	
		(−1.16)	
GDP Growth e~2			0.0000297**
			(1.97)
Constant	−1.859**	−1.796**	−1.612**
	(−2.44)	(−2.38)	(−2.19)
N	47	47	47
Model selection	Random effect	Random effect	Random effect

Notes: *t*-statistics in parentheses; *, **, and *** denotes significance levels of 10%, 5%, and 1%, respectively.

Appendix B

B.1. Structural Break Points Analysis Result

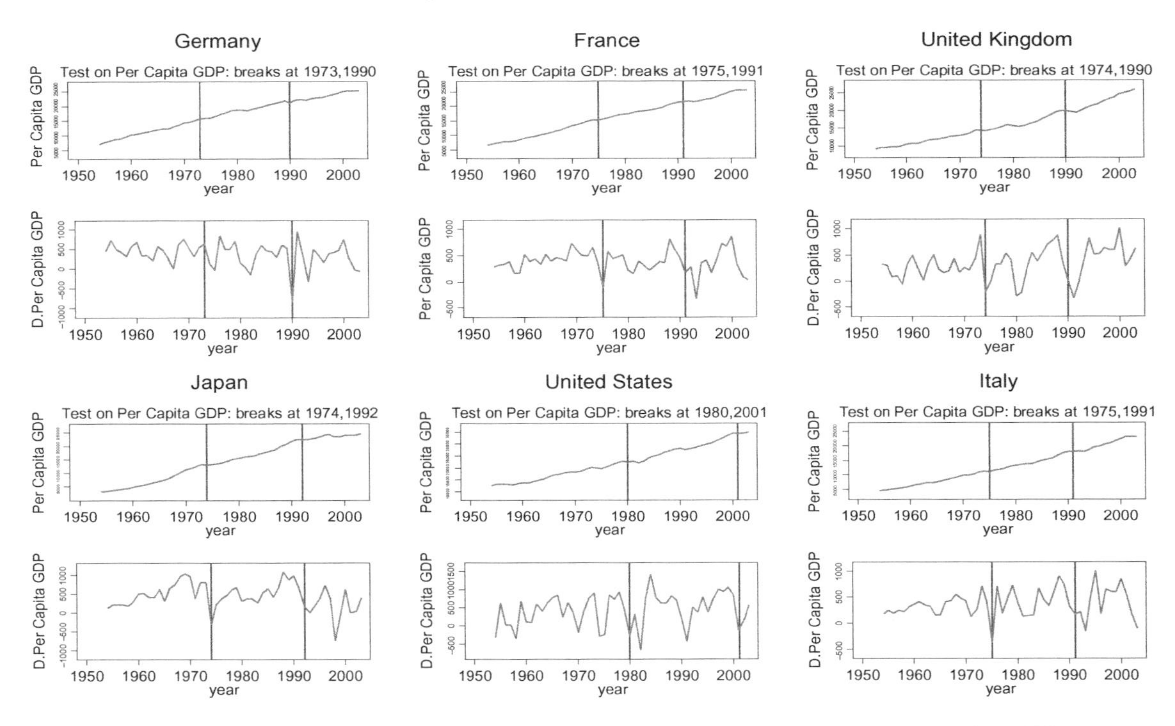

Figure B.1. Clemente–Montañes–Reyes structural break results of real GDP per capita (1956–2006).

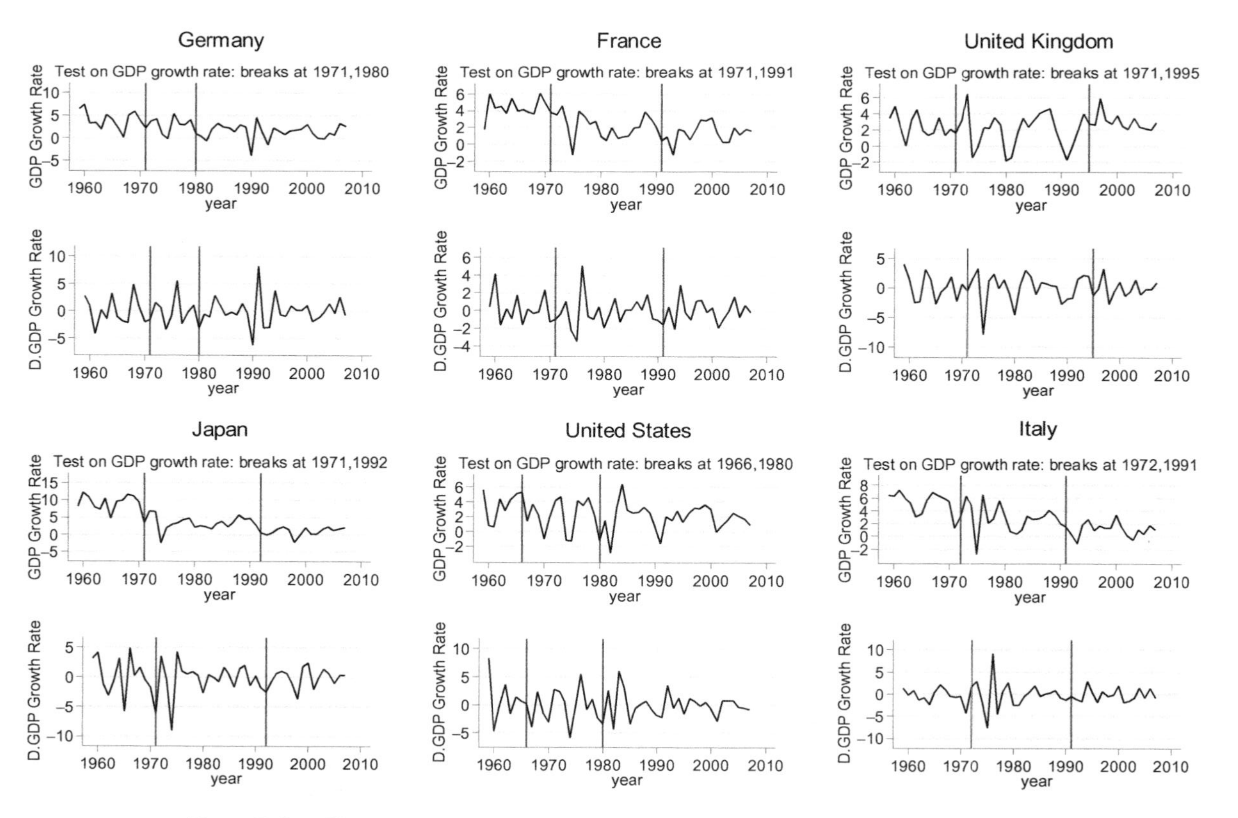

Figure B.2. Clemente–Montañes–Reyes structural break results of GDP (1956–2006).

B.2. BP Method

Table B.1. On real GDP per capita (1956–2006), global information criteria: France.

Breaks	# of coeffs.	Sum of sq. resids.	Log-L	Schwarz criterion	LWZ criterion
0	1	1.07E+10	−602.8599	19.15716	19.20295
1	3	2.56E+09	−563.5787	17.87448	18.01289
2	5	7.49E+08	−529.7817	16.79121	17.02373
3	7	3.84E+08	−511.4231	16.26935	16.59756*
4	9	3.14E+08	−505.8416	16.21211*	16.63776
5	11	2.83E+08	−503.0478	16.25624	16.78122

Notes: *Minimum information criterion values, Estimated break dates: [1 break: 1990], [2 breaks: 1987, 2004], [3 breaks: 1978, 1990, 2004], [4 breaks: 1975, 1987, 1995, 2004], [5 breaks: 1970, 1978, 1987, 1995, 2004].

Table B.2. On real GDP per capita (1956–2006), global information criteria: Germany.

Breaks	# of coeffs.	Sum of sq. resids.	Log-L	Schwarz criterion	LWZ criterion
0	1	8.47E+09	−492.5572	19.13815	19.18608
1	3	2.16E+09	−461.8305	17.9417	18.08707
2	5	6.97E+08	−436.359	16.97882	17.2239
3	7	4.55E+08	−426.739	16.72045	17.06775*
4	9	3.52E+08	−420.9637	16.63295*	17.08524
5	11	3.19E+08	−418.7764	16.70492	17.26529

Notes: *Minimum information criterion values, Estimated break dates: [1 break: 1990], [2 breaks: 1988, 2004], [3 breaks: 1978, 1990, 2006], [4 breaks: 1977, 1986, 1992, 2006], [5 breaks: 1977, 1986, 1992, 2001, 2007].

Table B.3. Real GDP per capita (1956–2006), global information criteria: Japan.

Breaks	# of coeffs.	Sum of sq. resids.	Log-L	Schwarz criterion	LWZ criterion
0	1	1.37E+10	−609.6623	19.40452	19.45031
1	3	1.60E+09	−550.7321	17.40733	17.54574
2	5	1.00E+09	−537.8348	17.08406	17.31657
3	7	6.83E+08	−527.2537	16.84501	17.17322*
4	9	5.68E+08	−522.1876	16.80651*	17.23216
5	11	5.34E+08	−520.4879	16.89042	17.41541

Notes: *Minimum information criterion values, Estimated break dates: [1 break: 1987], [2 breaks: 1985, 1993], [3 breaks: 1977, 1986, 1994], [4 breaks: 1977, 1986, 1994, 2007], [5 breaks: 1970, 1978, 1986, 1994, 2007].

Table B.4. Real GDP per capita (1956–2006), global information criteria: United Kingdom.

Breaks	# of coeffs.	Sum of sq. resids.	Log-L	Schwarz criterion	LWZ criterion
0	1	1.22E+10	−606.5696	19.29206	19.33785
1	3	2.83E+09	−566.3856	17.97655	18.11496
2	5	7.67E+08	−530.443	16.81526	17.04777
3	7	4.70E+08	−516.9847	16.47159	16.79981
4	9	2.63E+08	−500.9874	16.03559*	16.46125*
5	11	2.41E+08	−498.5699	16.0934	16.61839

Notes: *Minimum information criterion values, Estimated break dates: [1 break: 1996], [2 breaks: 1988, 2003], [3 breaks: 1979, 1990, 2003], [4 breaks: 1979, 1988, 1996, 2004], [5 breaks: 1971, 1979, 1988, 1996, 2004].

Table B.5. Real GDP per capita (1956–2006), global information criteria: United States.

Breaks	# of coeffs.	Sum of sq. resids.	Log-L	Schwarz criterion	LWZ criterion
0	1	1.50E+10	−612.1471	19.49488	19.54067
1	3	3.38E+09	−571.2055	18.15181	18.29022
2	5	1.26E+09	−543.9847	17.30769	17.5402
3	7	6.73E+08	−526.8225	16.82933	17.15754
4	9	3.92E+08	−511.9984	16.43599	16.86165
5	11	3.06E+08	−505.1445	16.33248*	16.85747*

Notes: *Minimum information criterion values, Estimated break dates: [1 break: 1993], [2 breaks: 1984, 2000], [3 breaks: 1981, 1994, 2004], [4 breaks: 1978, 1988, 1997, 2005], [5 breaks: 1973, 1981, 1989, 1997, 2005].

Table B.6. Real GDP per capita (1956–2006), global information criteria: Italy.

Breaks	# of coeffs.	Sum of sq. resids.	Log-L	Schwarz criterion	LWZ criterion
0	1	5.91E+09	−586.5764	18.56503	18.61082
1	3	9.50E+08	−536.3138	16.88302	17.02144
2	5	3.61E+08	−509.7435	16.06255	16.29507
3	7	1.75E+08	−489.8479	15.4848	15.81301
4	9	1.16E+08	−478.5368	15.21921*	15.64486*
5	11	1.09E+08	−476.7256	15.29906	15.82405

Notes: *Minimum information criterion values, Estimated break dates: [1 break: 1990], [2 breaks: 1985, 1997], [3 breaks: 1982, 1990, 2000], [4 breaks: 1980, 1988, 1996, 2004], [5 breaks: 1972, 1980, 1988, 1996, 2004].

Table B.7. On GDP (1956–2006): France.

Breaks	# of coeffs.	Sum of sq. resids.	Log-L	Schwarz criterion	LWZ criterion
0	1	184.348	−105.1334	1.362094	1.408734
1	3	91.04351	−87.14342	0.810796*	0.951932*
2	5	80.04151	−83.85922	0.836193	1.073564
3	7	78.63798	−83.40811	0.972691	1.308189
4	9	77.41865	−83.00962	1.111254	1.546945
5	11	77.17715	−82.92995	1.262319	1.800475

Notes: *Minimum information criterion values, Estimated break dates: [1 break: 1974], [2 breaks: 1974, 2002], [3 breaks: 1974, 1991, 2002], [4 breaks: 1974, 1981, 1994, 2001], [5 breaks: 1967, 1974, 1981, 1994, 2001].

Table B.8. On GDP (1956–2006): Germany.

Breaks	# of coeffs.	Sum of sq. resids.	Log-L	Schwarz criterion	LWZ criterion
0	1	246.4933	−112.5413	1.652604	1.699244
1	3	191.5028	−106.1043	1.554361*	1.695497*
2	5	187.0759	−105.5079	1.685162	1.922532
3	7	184.4807	−105.1517	1.825381	2.160878
4	9	183.2152	−104.9762	1.972687	2.408379
5	11	182.7498	−104.9113	2.124333	2.66249

Notes: *Minimum information criterion values, Estimated break dates: [1 break: 1980], [2 breaks: 1971, 1980], [3 breaks: 1971, 1980, 1990], [4 breaks: 1971, 1980, 1994, 2001], [5 breaks: 1971, 1980, 1987, 1994, 2001].

Table B.9. On GDP (1956–2006): Italy.

Breaks	# of coeffs.	Sum of sq. resids.	Log-L	Schwarz criterion	LWZ criterion
0	1	358.5708	−122.0985	2.027395	2.074035
1	3	216.0399	−109.1786	1.674921	1.816058*
2	5	177.2838	−104.137	1.631399*	1.86877
3	7	165.5715	−102.3941	1.71724	2.052737
4	9	161.5897	−101.7734	1.847087	2.282778
5	11	163.9243	−102.1391	2.01562	2.553776

Notes: *Minimum information criterion values, Estimated break dates: [1 break: 1975], [2 breaks: 1975, 2002], [3 breaks: 1971, 1990, 2002], [4 breaks: 1971, 1981, 1991, 2002], [5 breaks: 1968, 1975, 1984, 1991, 2002].

Table B.10. On GDP (1956–2006): Japan.

Breaks	# of coeffs.	Sum of sq. resids.	Log-L	Schwarz criterion	LWZ criterion
0	1	765.0719	−141.4235	2.785239	2.831879
1	3	276.6474	−115.4843	1.922202	2.063339
2	5	207.8931	−108.1984	1.790671*	2.028042*
3	7	204.3516	−107.7603	1.927679	2.263176
4	9	203.7105	−107.6802	2.078726	2.514417
5	11	203.5024	−107.6541	2.231893	2.77005

Notes: *Minimum information criterion values, Estimated break dates: [1 break: 1974], [2 breaks: 1971, 1992], [3 breaks: 1971, 1985, 1992], [4 breaks: 1971, 1985, 1992, 2000], [5 breaks: 1971, 1978, 1985, 1992, 2000].

Table B.11. On GDP (1956–2006): United Kingdom.

Breaks	# of coeffs.	Sum of sq. resids.	Log-L	Schwarz criterion	LWZ criterion
0	1	217.904	−109.3977	1.529324*	1.575964*
1	3	200.519	−107.2775	1.600367	1.741504
2	5	188.8951	−105.7547	1.694839	1.93221
3	7	174.8968	−103.7913	1.772033	2.10753
4	9	168.4022	−102.8264	1.888381	2.324073
5	11	154.9765	−100.7078	1.959488	2.497645

Notes: *Minimum information criterion values, Estimated break dates: [1 break: 2004], [2 breaks: 1994, 2004], [3 breaks: 1974, 1983, 2004], [4 breaks: 1974, 1982, 1994, 2004], [5 breaks: 1974, 1982, 1989, 1996, 2004].

Table B.12. On GDP (1956–2006): United States.

Breaks	# of coeffs.	Sum of sq. resids.	Log-L	Schwarz criterion	LWZ criterion
0	1	231.7524	−110.9689	1.590938*	1.637578*
1	3	208.2621	−108.2436	1.638256	1.779392
2	5	199.4844	−107.1456	1.749384	1.986754
3	7	189.0399	−105.7742	1.849795	2.185292
4	9	181.5329	−104.741	1.963463	2.399155
5	11	178.4659	−104.3064	2.100613	2.638769

Notes: *Minimum information criterion values, Estimated break dates: [1 break: 2001], [2 breaks: 1967, 2001], [3 breaks: 1974, 1983, 2001], [4 breaks: 1974, 1983, 1990, 2001], [5 breaks: 1967, 1974, 1983, 1990, 2001].

B.3. EEMD

B.3.1. *EEMD result*

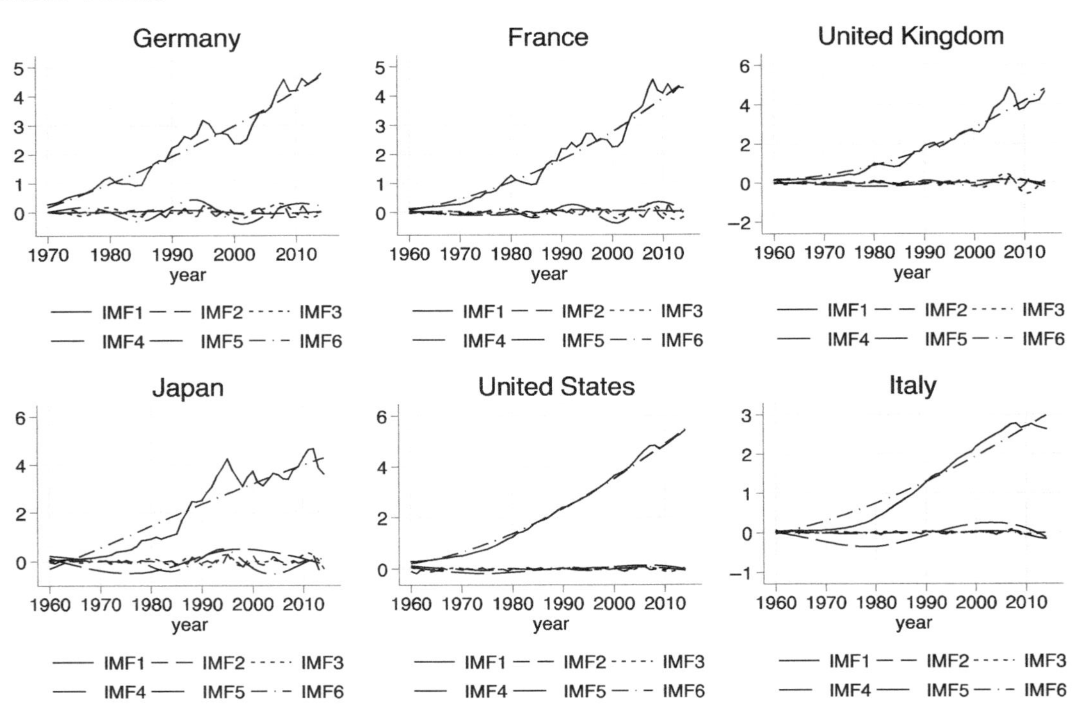

Figure B.3. The EEMD on per capita GDP of Germany, France, England, and Japan.

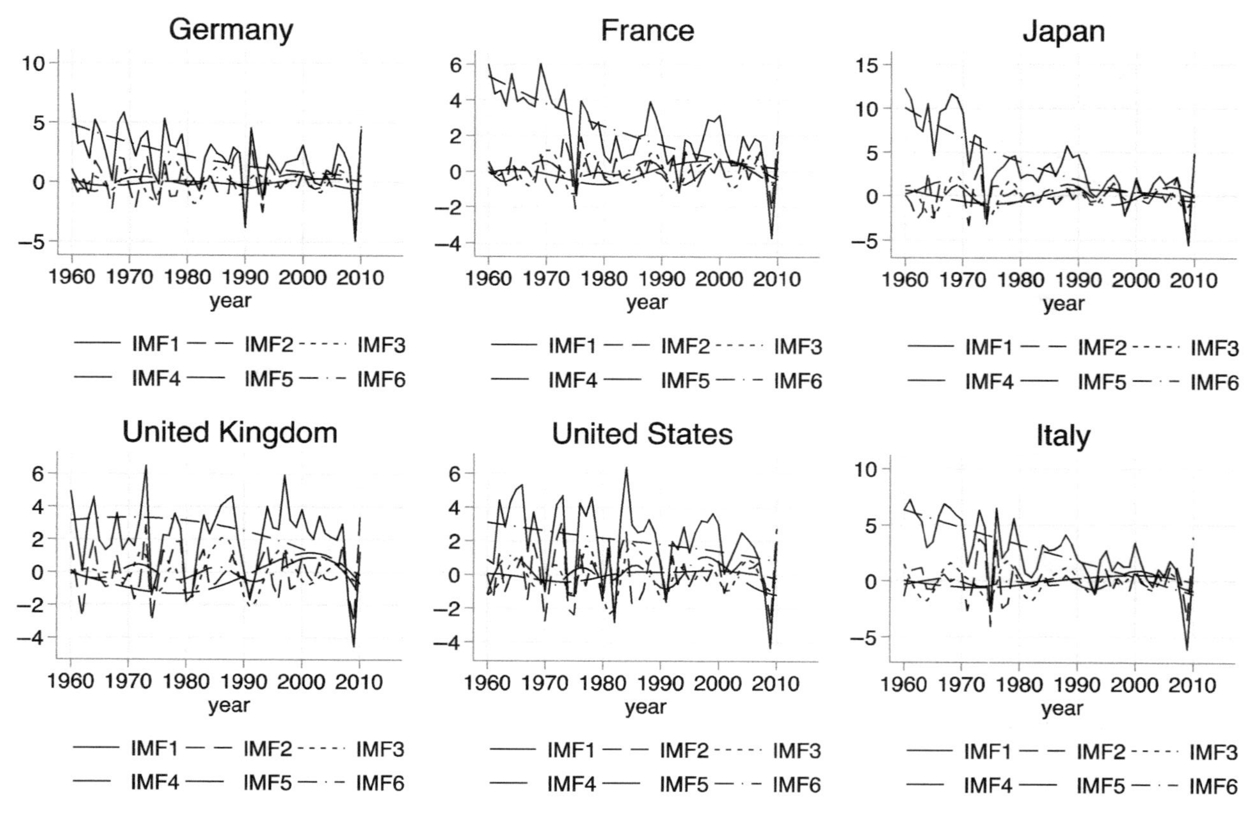

Figure B.4. The EEMD on GDP growth rate of Germany, France, England, and Japan.

B.3.2. *The EEMD series of selected countries and the regression result of government turnover and control variables*

Table B.13. The EEMD series of Japan per capita GDP and the regression result of government turnover and control variables.

	imf1	imf2	imf3	imf4	imf5	imf6
Number of changes in government per year	0.0875*	−0.0473	0.0182	0.0703*	0.0155*	0.000230
	(1.91)	(−1.58)	(0.53)	(2.13)	(1.99)	(0.67)
New ideological composition of cabinet	−0.169	−0.0199	−0.0971	−0.0699	−0.0137	0.000341
	(−1.31)	(−0.23)	(−1.00)	(−0.75)	(−0.62)	(0.35)
Party of chief executive length of time in office	0.0135**	0.00538	−0.00138	0.0101**	0.00237**	0.0000200
	(2.51)	(1.53)	(−0.34)	(2.59)	(2.58)	(0.50)
Regime durability	−0.0750	−0.0158	−0.0990	−0.0539	0.0441***	0.0823***
	(−0.95)	(−0.31)	(−1.67)	(−0.95)	(3.28)	(139.78)
University students	−0.00928	−0.00702	−0.0159*	0.0112	−0.00390*	0.000387***
	(−0.83)	(−0.96)	(−1.90)	(1.39)	(−2.05)	(−4.65)
Urbanization	−22.42	−6.960	5.988	−17.40	−8.588*	1.180***
	(−0.84)	(−0.40)	(0.30)	(−0.90)	(−1.88)	(5.91)
Population size	1.00e−08	1.73e−08	1.81e−08	−7.28e−09	−1.68e−09	−1.01e−10
	(0.64)	(1.69)	(1.54)	(−0.64)	(−0.63)	(−0.86)

(Continued)

Table B.13. *(Continued)*

	imf1	imf2	imf3	imf4	imf5	imf6
Exports	0.0000174***	0.00000273**	0.00000425***	0.00000819***	0.00000164***	4.27e–08***
	(12.90)	(3.09)	(4.18)	(8.39)	(7.10)	(4.23)
Inflation	–0.0302	–0.00409	–0.0113	0.00334	0.0000996	–0.000377*
	(–1.31)	(–0.27)	(–0.65)	(0.20)	(0.03)	(–2.20)
Governmental revenue	–0.0441	–0.0151	0.00333	–0.0426	–0.0103	–0.000716
	(–0.60)	(–0.31)	(0.06)	(–0.80)	(–0.83)	(–1.31)
Political globalization	0.00202	–0.0187	–0.0404	0.0378	0.00983*	0.000424*
	(0.07)	(–0.94)	(–1.77)	(1.72)	(1.89)	(1.87)
Economic globalization	0.00184	–0.00978**	–0.00177	0.00678	0.00120	0.0000907*
	(0.33)	(–2.64)	(–0.42)	(1.66)	(1.24)	(2.15)
Constant	14.41	4.201	–1.059	10.05	3.575*	–1.503***
	(1.27)	(0.57)	(–0.12)	(1.23)	(1.84)	(–17.73)
N	24	24	24	24	24	24
*r*2	0.996	0.772	0.847	0.967	0.999	1.000
*r*2_*a*	0.992	0.523	0.680	0.931	0.998	1.000
F	237.5	3.102	5.077	26.86	794.8	1097162.1

Notes: *t*-statistics in parentheses; *, **, and *** denotes significance levels of 10%, 5%, and 1%, respectively.

Table B.14. The EEMD series of England per capita GDP and the regression result of government turnover and control variables.

	imf1	imf2	imf3	imf4	imf5	imf6
Number of changes in government per year	0.0414	0.0320	0.0227	0.0103	−0.000589	−0.00256
	(1.22)	(1.39)	(0.96)	(0.57)	(−0.62)	(−1.30)
New ideological composition of cabinet	−0.0285	0.0410	−0.00927	−0.0685*	−0.00226	0.00983**
	(−0.48)	(1.03)	(−0.23)	(−2.18)	(−1.37)	(2.89)
Party of chief executive length of time in office	−0.0222**	−0.0104*	−0.00803	−0.00148	−0.000667**	−0.00222***
	(−2.64)	(−1.83)	(−1.38)	(−0.33)	(−2.83)	(−4.56)
Regime durability	0.0610	0.0318	−0.0300	−0.0367	0.00709***	0.0720***
	(1.27)	(0.98)	(−0.91)	(−1.43)	(5.27)	(25.95)
University students	−0.0108	−0.0721	0.0228	0.0412	0.00729***	0.0192***
	(−0.17)	(−1.67)	(0.52)	(1.21)	(4.08)	(5.20)
Urbanization	13.71	3.703	6.817	13.79***	−1.229***	−4.080***
	(1.72)	(0.69)	(1.24)	(3.24)	(−5.51)	(−8.86)
Population size	2.91e−09	4.02e−08	−1.68e−08	1.28e−08	−2.62e−09	−1.45e−08***
	(0.04)	(0.86)	(−0.35)	(0.35)	(−1.36)	(−3.63)
Exports	0.00000669**	0.00000469**	0.00000205	−0.00000112	6.46e−08	0.000000527***
	(2.50)	(2.58)	(1.10)	(−0.78)	(0.86)	(3.39)

(Continued)

Table B.14. (*Continued*)

	imf1	imf2	imf3	imf4	imf5	imf6
Inflation	0.00824	−0.0127**	0.00618	0.0116**	0.000957***	−0.000433
	(0.97)	(−2.21)	(1.05)	(2.54)	(4.01)	(−0.88)
Governmental revenue	−0.0290*	0.00826	0.00321	−0.0226**	−0.00287***	−0.00116
	(−1.85)	(0.78)	(0.30)	(−2.70)	(−6.56)	(−1.28)
Political globalization	−0.0628**	−0.0339*	−0.0208	−0.0353**	−0.00213**	0.00306*
	(−2.31)	(−1.84)	(−1.11)	(−2.42)	(−2.78)	(1.94)
Economic globalization	−0.0221	0.0195	−0.0210	−0.0223*	−0.000716	0.00161
	(−1.03)	(1.34)	(−1.42)	(−1.94)	(−1.19)	(1.30)
Constant	−10.50**	−7.206**	0.436	−4.786*	0.457***	−2.748***
	(−2.29)	(−2.32)	(0.14)	(−1.94)	(3.55)	(−10.33)
N	24	24	24	24	24	24
*r*2	0.995	0.709	0.831	0.888	1.000	1.000
*r*2_*a*	0.990	0.391	0.647	0.766	0.999	1.000
F	191.5	2.229	4.516	7.275	3041.2	45055.0

Notes: *t*-statistics in parentheses; *, **, and *** denotes significance levels of 10%, 5%, and 1%, respectively.

Table B.15. The EEMD series of America per capita GDP and the regression result of government turnover and control variables.

	imf1	imf2	imf3	imf4	imf5	imf6
Number of changes in government per year	0.0150	0.0142	−0.00151	0.00552	0.00441	0.00189
	(0.66)	(0.61)	(−0.10)	(0.58)	(1.71)	(0.39)
Party of chief executive length of time in office	−0.00286	−0.00150	0.00304	−0.00115	0.00129**	0.000172
	(−0.67)	(−0.34)	(1.05)	(−0.65)	(2.67)	(0.19)
Regime durability	0.0826***	−0.00955	−0.00630	0.00643	0.0160***	0.0783***
	(7.88)	(−0.89)	(−0.88)	(1.47)	(13.44)	(35.43)
University students	10.00**	−4.495	−4.554	4.539**	−0.680	12.99***
	(2.27)	(−0.99)	(−1.51)	(2.46)	(−1.35)	(13.96)
Urbanization	2.47e−10	3.68e−10	2.06e−09	−1.57e−09	−2.28e−10	−7.51e−10
	(0.07)	(0.10)	(0.88)	(−1.10)	(−0.59)	(−1.04)
Population size	0.00000000845**	0.00000000726*	0.00000000488*	−0.00000000269*	−0.00000000111**	0.00000000197**
	(2.26)	(1.89)	(1.91)	(−1.72)	(−2.61)	(2.49)
Exports	−0.00194	−0.0102	−0.00100	0.00678**	−0.000653	0.00224
	(−0.30)	(−1.51)	(−0.22)	(2.47)	(−0.87)	(1.62)

(*Continued*)

Table B.15. (*Continued*)

	imf1	imf2	imf3	imf4	imf5	imf6
Inflation	−0.0130	−0.0177	−0.00119	−0.000307	−0.00192	−0.00447
	(−0.52)	(−0.68)	(−0.07)	(−0.03)	(−0.67)	(−0.84)
Governmental revenue	−0.00746	0.00438	−0.00229	0.0000849	0.0000786	−0.00783**
	(−0.54)	(0.31)	(−0.24)	(0.01)	(0.05)	(−2.68)
Political globalization	−0.0355***	−0.00743	0.00227	−0.0151***	−0.00248***	−0.00924***
	(−4.70)	(−0.96)	(0.44)	(−4.79)	(−2.88)	(−5.80)
Economic globalization	−16.55***	5.782	3.831	−2.787*	−2.020***	−20.14***
	(−4.38)	(1.49)	(1.49)	(−1.76)	(−4.70)	(−25.28)
N	32	32	32	32	32	32
*r*2	0.999	0.248	0.419	0.795	0.998	1.000
*r*2_*a*	0.998	−0.110	0.143	0.698	0.997	1.000
F	1621.6	0.692	1.516	8.163	910.6	30115.3

Notes: *t*-statistics in parentheses; *, **, and *** denotes significance levels of 10%, 5%, and 1%, respectively.

Table B.16. The EEMD series of Germany per capita GDP and the regression result of government turnover and control variables.

	imf1	imf2	imf3	imf4	imf5	imf6
Number of changes in government per year	1.125	0.951	0.236	−0.0148	−0.00828	0.000474
	(1.48)	(1.12)	(0.6)	(−0.23)	(−0.86)	(0.38)
Party of chief executive length of time in office	−0.18	−0.12	−0.0525	0.00314	0.00258	−0.0000586
	(−1.59)	(−0.96)	(−0.91)	(0.33)	(1.81)	(−0.32)
Regime durability	−0.523	−0.404	−0.121	−0.0158	0.0662***	−0.0428***
	(−1.02)	(−0.71)	(−0.46)	(−0.36)	(10.16)	(−50.78)
Urbanization	−2961.8*	−1142.9	−1371.9*	−447.7***	−35.57*	16.44***
	(−2.21)	(−0.77)	(−2.00)	(−3.90)	(−2.10)	(7.49)
Population size	−1.3E−06	−1.2E−06	−2.1E−07	0.000000313*	−7.47e−08**	−2.69e−08***
	(−0.70)	(−0.59)	(−0.21)	(1.94)	(−3.13)	(−8.71)
Exports	0.0000248**	1.41E−05	0.00000991*	1.19E−06	−0.000000291**	−2.62E−08
	(2.55)	(1.31)	(1.99)	(1.43)	(−2.37)	(−1.65)
Inflation	−0.326	−0.527	0.359	−0.0917*	−0.00588	0.00168*
	(−0.69)	(−1.01)	(1.49)	(−2.29)	(−0.99)	(2.18)
Constant	2267.8**	934.8	1015.3*	301.6***	31.83**	−8.520***
	(2.32)	(0.86)	(2.03)	(3.61)	(2.58)	(−5.33)
N	16	16	16	16	16	16
*r*2	0.753	0.632	0.574	0.977	0.997	1
*r*2_*a*	0.537	0.311	0.201	0.957	0.995	1
F	3.482	1.966	1.538	48.6	453.8	37831.1

Notes: *t*-statistics in parentheses; *, **, and *** denotes significance levels of 10%, 5%, and 1%, respectively.

Table B.17. The EEMD series of Italy GDP growth rate and the regression result of government turnover and control variables.

	imf1	imf2	imf3	imf4	imf5	imf6
Number of changes in government per year	−0.00296	0.00593	−0.00295	0.000419	0.00341**	0.00163
	(−0.47)	(0.54)	(−0.57)	(0.22)	(3.06)	(1.16)
New ideological composition of cabinet	−0.00506	−0.00791	−0.00434	−0.00156	0.00295	0.00134
	(−0.47)	(−0.43)	(−0.49)	(−0.48)	(1.56)	(0.56)
Party of chief executive length of time in office	−0.0000217	−0.00219*	−0.000498	0.000304	0.000528***	−0.000159
	(−0.03)	(−1.82)	(−0.86)	(1.45)	(4.28)	(−1.03)
Regime durability	0.0930***	−0.00513	−0.0119	0.00608	0.0281***	0.0606***
	(7.33)	(−0.23)	(−1.13)	(1.59)	(12.46)	(21.38)
University students	0.00238	0.00469	−0.00243	−0.00368	0.00169	0.0114***
	(0.25)	(0.29)	(−0.31)	(−1.30)	(1.01)	(5.42)
Urbanization	−24.30***	1.059	0.223	−2.233	−16.19***	−5.615***
	(−5.59)	(0.14)	(0.06)	(−1.70)	(−20.97)	(−5.78)
Population size	−4.66e−09	−2.30e−08	1.52e−08	−8.88e−10	−1.43e−08***	−7.32e−09
	(−0.25)	(−0.72)	(0.99)	(−0.16)	(−4.38)	(−1.78)
Exports	0.000000747	0.000000690	0.000000459	−0.000000237	0.000000255*	−0.000000246
	(1.05)	(0.56)	(0.77)	(−1.10)	(2.02)	(−1.55)

Inflation	0.00398*	0.00125	0.000872	0.000178	0.000863**	0.000922*
	(1.86)	(0.34)	(0.49)	(0.27)	(2.26)	(1.92)
Governmental revenue	0.000669	–0.000518	0.00552	0.00271	0.00290***	–0.00341**
	(0.13)	(–0.06)	(1.30)	(1.76)	(3.21)	(–3.00)
Political globalization	–0.000588	–0.00305	0.00251	0.00000245	0.00201**	–0.000483
	(–0.12)	(–0.36)	(0.62)	(0.00)	(2.32)	(–0.44)
Economic globalization	0.00159	0.000410	–0.00451	–0.00119	0.000426	–0.000478
	(0.40)	(0.06)	(–1.37)	(–0.99)	(0.61)	(–0.54)
Constant	13.48***	0.666	–0.443	1.484*	9.992***	2.687***
	(5.39)	(0.15)	(–0.21)	(1.97)	(22.52)	(4.81)
N	23	23	23	23	23	23
*r*2	1.000	0.384	0.646	0.967	1.000	1.000
*r*2_a	0.999	–0.355	0.222	0.927	1.000	1.000
F	2534.2	0.520	1.523	24.38	7795.0	22059.2

Notes: *t*-statistics in parentheses; *, **, and *** denotes significance levels of 10%, 5%, and 1%, respectively.

B.3.3. *Panel data result*

Table B.18. The EEMD series of Italy per capita GDP and the regression result of government turnover and control variables.

	imf1	imf2	imf3	imf4	imf5	imf6
Number of changes in government per year	0.000844	−0.00799	0.0133	−0.000531	−0.00157	−0.00697
	(0.02)	(−0.64)	(0.94)	(−0.02)	(−0.09)	(−0.27)
New ideological composition of cabinet	0.0805	0.0237	0.0173	−0.0432	0.0364	0.0498
	(0.82)	(1.04)	(0.67)	(−0.96)	(1.09)	(1.07)
Party of chief executive length of time in office	−0.0125***	−0.0000432	−0.00217**	−0.00579***	−0.00459***	−0.000500
	(−3.03)	(−0.04)	(−1.98)	(−3.04)	(−3.24)	(−0.25)
Regime durability	−0.0113**	0.00260**	0.00177	−0.00941***	−0.00706***	0.000889
	(−2.30)	(2.25)	(1.35)	(−4.13)	(−4.16)	(0.38)
University students	−0.0164***	0.000719	0.00147*	−0.00399***	−0.00999***	−0.00487***
	(−5.07)	(0.95)	(1.72)	(−2.67)	(−9.01)	(−3.14)
Urbanization	1.355	−0.422	−0.0661	1.633***	0.297	−0.0415
	(1.19)	(−1.58)	(−0.22)	(3.11)	(0.76)	(−0.08)
Population size	9.17e−09**	−2.01e−09**	−2.08e−09*	6.55e−09***	7.42e−09***	−9.38e−10
	(2.19)	(−2.05)	(−1.86)	(3.38)	(5.16)	(−0.47)

Exports	0.00000428***	0.000000306**	0.000000391**	−0.000000217	4.13e−08	0.00000386***
	(6.69)	(2.04)	(2.30)	(−0.74)	(0.19)	(12.59)
Inflation	−0.0329***	0.00118	0.00200	0.00929**	−0.00654**	−0.0387***
	(−3.41)	(0.52)	(0.78)	(2.09)	(−1.98)	(−8.37)
Governmental revenue	−0.0675***	0.00641	0.000347	−0.0220***	−0.0164***	−0.0359***
	(−3.89)	(1.58)	(0.08)	(−2.76)	(−2.77)	(−4.33)
Political globalization	0.0450***	−0.00497	−0.00465	0.0188***	0.0245***	0.00987
	(3.21)	(−1.51)	(−1.25)	(2.91)	(5.11)	(1.47)
Economic globalization	−0.00994	−0.00337**	−0.00293	0.00374	0.000537	−0.00802**
	(−1.48)	(−2.14)	(−1.64)	(1.20)	(0.23)	(−2.49)
Constant	1.760	0.529**	0.461	−1.383***	−0.655*	2.876***
	(1.61)	(2.07)	(1.59)	(−2.75)	(−1.75)	(5.50)
N	103	103	103	103	103	103

Note: *, **, and *** denotes significance levels of 10%, 5%, and 1%, respectively.

Chapter 3

Does Ideology Matter? Political Parties and Social Security Policies in Democracies*

Based on the fixed effects model, this chapter explores the impact of political parties' position on the left–right ideology scale on social security policy outputs by analyzing the panel data of 23 countries from 1960 to 2014. The findings, complementing the traditional opinion that left-wing incumbency tends to increase social security expenditure, indicate that in some democracies, right-wing incumbency inclines to spend more on social security. In addition, we point out that the impacts of the left–right scale on social security expenditure were different before and after the revolutions of 1989, and that they are also different in the welfare states of high level and those of low level. Finally, the implications of our results for political theories and political practice are discussed. The validity of these results is verified by the robustness test.

1. Introduction: Ideology and Social Policy

A political party is an important part of modern political activities, and studies of its role and impact on social and economic policies have been thriving in recent decades. The concept of ideology of political party,

*I'm grateful to Luyue Xie for remarkable research assistance.

which is regarded as the idea that political opinions and attitudes are linked together in a modern state, has been theorized as particularly essential for the democracies. The left–right cleavage of parties, on one hand, reflects fundamental and fierce competitions for party government that is a hot area of research, and on the other hand, embeds itself in the influences of ideological differences with scant attention from scholars.

Traditional theories of partisan politics assume a linear and coherent relationship between the type of party in power (e.g., social-democratic or conservative) and policy outputs (Budge, 2001; Klingemann, 2006). In some of these studies, different political parties can often respond to their supporting coalitions differently when initiating public policies (Butler, Volden, Dynes, & Shor, 2017). For example, researchers have argued that, with left-wing parties in power, the income gap is inversely proportional to the economic growth rate, while with right-wing parties in power, it is in proportion to the economic growth rate (Bjørnskov, 2008). Previous studies have often been conducted on the basis of the power resource theory or the "parties-matter" hypothesis (Birchfield & Crepaz, 1998; Bradley & Stephens, 2001; Hicks & Swank, 1992; Rueda, 2007), and also have already concluded that the left–right cleavage matters for various policy outputs (Schmidt, 1996).

The importance of ideology has been highlighted in the wide range of empirical researches showing how ideological structures significantly affect social policies and individual behaviors (Carmines & D'Amico, 2015; Jost, 2006). For instance, it is long regarded that left-wing parties have spent more on social welfare and have reduced the levels of economic inequality and poverty, however, West European right-wing parties have received a great deal of attention over the past two decades thanks to their electoral success (Arzheimer & Carter, 2006). In the study of the Nordic countries, Carsten Jenson convincingly argued that right-wing parties also increase social welfare expenditure to win support from voters (Jensen, 2010).

In recent years, some studies suggest that policy differences among various parties are narrowing with socio-economic development (Schumacher, 2015); and the traditional idea about the social–economic spillover effect of the left–right scale is facing many severe challenges in academic studies. Häusermann, Picot, and Geering (2013) have pointed out that over the past 10 years, an increasing number of studies have shown that party politics often shapes social policies in ways that differ from traditional hypotheses and mechanisms implied by the traditional partisan politics or parties-matter theory. Meanwhile, the majority of conclusions in current empirical studies are inconsistent and even contradictory to relatively older studies (Afonso, 2015; Afonso & Papadopoulos, 2013; Bay, Finseraas, & Pedersen, 2013; Han, 2015; Hicks, 2011; Lange, Festenstein, & Smith, 2012; Neumayer, 2003; Williams, 2006).

In short, early data suggested some clear relevance between ideological difference and policy choice difference. However, with the development of welfare state retrenchment in the globalization age, the debate on the relevance of political parties and ideology is still far from settled (Starke, 2006). So there remains a need for further explore on the influence of ideology on social public policy in some countries based on updated data.

To further test the impact of left-wing or right-wing parties on social policy outputs, we observe the change of social security transfers as a percentage of GDP under the contexts of different parties in power. In this process, the method we employ is that of conducting a quantitative analysis based on the panel data of 23 countries from 1960 to 2014. Based on the fixed effects model, the chapter builds its conclusion after authors' scrutiny on the data. The conclusion of this chapter seriously complemented traditional ideas that are seemingly convincing in the past to some extent. Additionally, using the revolutions of 1989 as the demarcation point, the authors comprehensively analyze the differences between the impact of left-wing and right-wing parties on social security policies before and after that year. The findings indicate that the impact is more complex but is fading away, because the ideologies of the parties are laying some real points of convergence.

The other parts of our chapter are organized as follows. Section 2 reviews the relevant literature. The data description and research design are provided in Section 3. Sections 4 and 5 present the regression results of the panel data and robustness test. Finally, this chapter is concluded in Section 5.

2. Ideology and Its Influences on Social Security Policy

2.1. *Party ideology*

Party ideology, as an abstract concept, encompasses a collection of ideas, opinions and attitudes directly connected with the politics and economy. The term "ideology" itself derives from the early 19th century; however, the close integration of the modern politics and ideology is one of the important traits in our society. History since the early 20th century has shown that political ideology plays a critical role in the ebb and flow of different parties. Ideological conflicts even trigger wars and governance crises at home and abroad (Kane, 2007; Moses, 2013; Steinberger, 1985). It is no exaggeration to say that, in the whole previous century, the history of modern political and economic change is the very history of party ideologies' competition, bankruptcy, reconstruction, and renovation.

In democracies, party ideology is of critical importance for the rise and fall of these countries through election campaigns. Potrafke (2010) argued that left-wing and right-wing parties have different attitudes towards the role of government in the market and the basic elements of political order. Rudolph and Evans (2005) also contended that ideology has an effect on their attitudes towards the distribution and redistribution of national income, while Hooghe, Marks, and Wilson (2002) all held the view that ideological fervors of left-wing and right-wing parties are closely related to their positions in European integration. To put it simply, ideology imperceptibly impacts on governments in an all-round way.

After the revolutions of 1989, the debates about the end of history and the end of ideology fundamentally impacted on existing ideological labels. In particular, since the end of 20th century, a number of welfare states began to reduce welfare spending. In that case, scholars raised the following questions, would partisan politics cease to play a decisive role in policy-making and welfare spending? Should we give up the debate about the end of history and the end of ideology (Bell, 1962; Fukuyama, 2006; Hindess, 1996)? Has the impact of party ideologies on policies changed before and after the revolutions of 1989? These questions are still waiting to be answered by rigorous research results.

2.2. *Social security policy*

Public policy is determined and shaped by many factors (Busemeyer & Garritzmann, 2017; Persson & Tabellini, 2002; Radaelli, 1995). During the process of state building in the 20th century, many welfare states, which spend their large proportion of revenues on social security, have risen one after another. Various factors, of course, could result in the rise of these welfare states, including globalization, the development of information industry, the accumulation of government revenues, the end of Cold War, the institutional quality and the differences in parties.

Social security policy not only guarantees citizens a basic living and increases their happiness index, but also has an impact on the future social stratification and class mobility of a nation (Skocpol, 2000). Current studies have demonstrated that the public have different preferences over social security policies due to their various values (Feldman & Zaller, 1992). Ideologies of political parties are more likely to influence public policy debates and social policy strategies that are developed to address "social problems" (George & Wilding, 1985; Mizrahi & Davis, 2008). Specifically, different ideologies of political parties also greatly influence the formulation and modification of social security rules, and are crucial for social security financing, via voting and discussions in parliaments.

2.3. *Ideology and social security policy*

In terms of the impact of party differences on social policies, although the impact of leadership change in democracies is more subtle, a new leader and the supporting coalition still exert a significant effects on policy change. In a series of publications, Valerie Bunce analyzed in detail the impact of elite turnover on policy change in democratic and communist countries (Bunce, 1980, 2014). In contrast, Brunk and Minehart (1984) found that leadership turnover has no short-run impact on the level of budget changes and little long-run impact as a leader, which is periodically reelected in seven western democracies.

Generally, studies on the relationship between party politics and social security policies can be divided into two groups regarding their different research approaches. The first research approach is more traditional and has been dominated by the party politics theory that different parties represent interests of different voters and social policy outputs are the products of political parties' response to voters, political ideologies and political competition. For example, after analyzing the data on social unemployment, inflation, and political macroeconomic goals, it was found that different parties always have different policy preferences, with the left-wing Social Democratic Party preferring policies that are related to the interests of working-class and under-privileged voters. Van Kersbergen (2003) also argued that low-income and working-class voters are directly and closely related to left-wing incumbency. In the study of welfare states, scholars have systematically explored the positions of six major ideological schools of thought towards the welfare states of today and the future: the New Right, the Middle Way, Democratic Socialism, Marxism, Feminism, and Greenism, and they have concluded that political ideologies play a pivotal role in the future of welfare states (George & Wilding, 1985).

Scholars also find that structural change is a major determinant of the extent of social protection. They suggest that overall spending is driven up by structural change. On the other hand, strong structural change has a negative influence on welfare entitlements measured by the net rate of sickness insurance. Partisan influence significantly affect the dynamics of the welfare state (Amable, Gatti, & Schumacher, 2006). In researches on less developed countries also suggests similar conclusion that more democratic nations spend a greater amount of money on social security and welfare, while leftist governments spend more on education (Ha, 2015).

The second approach used by scholars is that of a micro perspective, like the behaviors of parties and voters. At this stage, the traditional "parties-matter" hypothesis and power resources theory have been completely challenged, because the voter base has changed remarkably after the left-wing incumbency has attracted more middle class voters. Häusermann *et al.* (2013) revealed that party politics based on left-wing and right-wing ideologies face multiple difficulties at present. Studies on Europe have indicated that prolonged left-wing incumbency produces greater demand for social welfare and the formation of vested interest groups. Therefore, right-wing parties should pledge to spend more on social welfare than their left-wing counterparts if they intend to win elections (Jensen, 2010). Thus, right-wing parties will exert even more efforts in order to support social security than left-wing ones. Faced with such changes, some radical scholars have even claimed that party politics would not play a decisive role in studies on welfare states any longer (Allan & Scruggs, 2004).

For a government that seeks re-election, in order to enhance its prospects, the incumbent may pursue quite different policies in an election year. We can also find a significant partisan effect on policy outcomes in some OECD countries. Political budget cycle theory is used to explain this phenomenon, which contains the influence of different ideologies on policy outputs. (Alt & Lassen, 2006; Efthyvoulou, 2012; Klomp & Haan, 2013).

Previous scholars also noted factors that could impact on the influence of partisan effect on social security policy. Early in last century, based on her observation on British social security policy in 1980s, Lister (1991) noticed British government's ambivalent attitudes towards "the poor" revealed in the interplay between ideology and pragmatic politics (Lister, 2010). Many specifications of previous party-mattered theory compose the argument that the structural-institutional effect of embedded welfare state regimes mediates the partisan effect of parties in government (Bradley & Stephens, 2007; Esping-Andersen, 1990).

The above-mentioned contradictory studies have indicated that empirical studies still do not come to a consistent conclusion about the impact of left-wing and right-wing parties on social security policies. The relation between party ideology and social security policy is changing along the time as party politics are evolving. Thus there needs to be continuous investigation on this subject. In addition, due to difficulties in data acquisition, current studies have mainly conducted an analysis based on cross-sectional data rather than panel data from many countries. In contrast, this chapter uses panel data to further examine the impact of party politics on social security policies. First, the authors put forward the following hypothesis.

Hypothesis 1: Ceteris paribus, left-wing and right-wing parties in power have different influences over social security policies, which is either positive or negative.

With further analysis, we also find that current studies on different time periods have reached different conclusions about the impact of party politics. For instance, when studying the impact before the revolutions of 1989, we find these conclusions consistent. However, when studying its impact after the revolutions of 1989, the authors discover that they are diverse or even conflicting. Thus, it is reasonable to assume that the end of the Cold War reduced ideological conflicts between different political parties, and further lowered the impact of political parties on social security policies. On that basis, the authors advance a second hypothesis.

Hypothesis 2: Ceteris paribus, the positive or negative impact of different parties in power on social security policies are significant before 1989, while the impact is non-significant after 1989, which is either positive or negative.

3. Measuring the Impact of Ideology Turnover on Social Policy

3.1. *Data description*

The majority of data used in this study are from the Comparative Political Data Set (CPDS) (Armingeon *et al.*, 2016) and the Quality of Government (Dahlberg, Holmberg, Rothstein, Hartmann, & Svensson, 2016), which have been acknowledged as credible in academic circles (Layton-Henry, 2006; Lijphart, 2002; Boräng, Nistotskaya, & Xezonakis, 2017, Carbone & Pellegata, 2016, Rothstein, 2011). CPDS is a collection of political and institutional country-level data. Why did we choose CPDS as our core data set? Because with our knowledge, there are at least three databases containing information of leader turnover, Cross-National Time-Series Data Archive (Banks & Wilson, 2013), Change in Source of Leader Support (CHISOLS) Dataset (Mattes, Leeds, & Matsumura, 2016), and Archigos: A Database on Political Leaders (Goemans, Gleditsch, & Chiozza, 2009). Different from CPDS, these datasets only provide information about when a leader change occurs without coding the direction of that change, especially the ideology of the leader. However, CPDS consists of (mostly) annual data for 35 democratic OECD and/or EU-member countries for the period from 1960 to 2014. So it is suitable for cross-national, longitudinal, and pooled time-series analyses. With superior quality, these aforementioned data are used in numerous studies and published in various peer reviewed journals. To ensure the quality of the data used in this chapter, 12 countries were omitted from our study because large portions of their data (15% or more for any category or year) were missing, so our final sample consisted of the panel data of 23 developed democracies in the period from 1960 to 2014 (see details in Table A.1). Variable descriptions are provided in Tables 1 and 2.

The dependent variable in this chapter is social security transfers as a percentage of GDP, which is one of the most important factors reflecting social security policies and is widely used in many other research projects.

Table 1. Continuous variables descriptive statistics.

Variable name	Variable description	Mean	Maximum	Minimum	Std. dev.
sstran	Social security transfers as a percentage of GDP.	12.56	23.89	3.48	4.11
netu	Net union membership, in thousands.	3502.19	20880.00	52.40	4308.52
realgdpgr	Growth of real GDP, percent change from previous year.	2.95	13.20	–9.18	2.84
unemp	Unemployment rate, percentage of civilian labor force.	5.52	27.50	0.00	4.02
receipts	Total receipts (revenue) of general government as a percentage of GDP.	40.67	59.86	19.97	8.51
labfopar	Total labor force as a percentage of population 15–64 (participation rate).	72.16	109.81	55.44	7.96

Table 2. Categorical variables descriptive statistics.

Variable	Variable description	Percent (%)	Total (%)
	1 hegemony of right-wing (and center) parties (gov_left1 = 0)	41.21	
	2 dominance of right-wing (and center) parties (0<gov_ left1<= 33.33)	17.06	
Gov_party Cabinet composition (Schmidt-Index)	3 balance of power between left and right (33.33 <gov_left1 < 66.67)	17.9	100
	4 dominance of social-democratic and other left parties (66.67 <= gov_left1 <100)	8.07	
	5 hegemony of social-democratic and other left parties (gov_left = 100)	15.76	

The independent variable is the ideology of the ruling party, which is classified into five types based on Cabinet composition (Schmidt-Index). (Schmidt-Sørensen, 1992) To improve the accuracy of our model, we created dummy variables *party_j* (*j* = 1, 2,..., 5) according to the variable *gov_party*, with party 1 representing extreme right parties in power, party 2 being right-wing parties in power, party 3 presenting center parties in power, party 4 standing for left-wing parties in power and party 5 denoting extreme left parties in power.

$$\text{party}_1 = \begin{cases} 1, & \text{if extreme right} \\ 0, & \text{if not extreme right} \end{cases} \qquad \text{party}_4 = \begin{cases} 1, & \text{if left-wing} \\ 0, & \text{if not left-wing} \end{cases}$$

$$\text{party}_2 = \begin{cases} 1, & \text{if right-wing} \\ 0, & \text{if not right-wing} \end{cases} \qquad \text{party}_5 = \begin{cases} 1, & \text{if extreme left} \\ 0, & \text{if not extreme left} \end{cases}$$

$$\text{party}_3 = \begin{cases} 1, & \text{if center} \\ 0, & \text{if not center} \end{cases}$$

To ensure the reliability of the results, the authors took several factors as control variables, such as the scale of trade unions, the growth rate of GDP, government revenues, the unemployment rate, and aging population, which, as confirmed by recent studies via cross-national research, have an impact on the total expenditure on social welfare. (Finkelstein & Hambrick, 1990; Gasparyan, 2015; La Porta, Lopezdesilanes, Shleifer, & Vishny, 1999).

3.2. *Methods and stylized facts*

This chapter constructed the following equation to examine the earlier-mentioned hypotheses and to observe the effect of different ideological parties on social security policies:

$$\begin{aligned} \text{sstran}_{it} = {} & \text{cons}_i + \text{party\_j}_{it}\alpha_j + \text{netu}_{it}\beta_1 + \text{realgdpr}_{it}\beta_2 \\ & + \text{unemp}_{it}\beta_3 + \text{receipts}_{it}\beta_4 + \text{labfopar}_{it}\beta_5 + \text{u}_{it} \end{aligned} \tag{1}$$

where sstran, i.e., social security transfers as a percentage of GDP, is the explained variable; subscript *i* and *t* represent country and year respectively; is independent variables, which are dummy variables ($j = 1, 2, \ldots, 5$), reflecting that different parties are in power. Besides these variables, a number of control variables which reflect political and economic institutions are introduced: *netu* represents the net union membership; *realgdpr* stands for the growth of real GDP; *unemp* is the unemployment rate; receipts denotes the total receipts (revenue) of general government as a percentage of GDP; and *labfopar* presents the total labor force measured as a percentage of the population 15–64 (participation rate). *Cons* denotes a constant term, and u_{it} represents a traditional error term. Dummy variables are contained in this study and their number is always smaller than that of categories. To avoid the dummy variable trap and multicollinearity, the dummy variable of the center party (party3) is deleted in this model.

Before further analyzing the data, the authors first vividly describe the trends of social security transfers as a percentage of GDP in different countries in Figure 1. As can be seen, social security expenditures in New Zealand, Japan, Germany, Luxembourg, Iceland, and Switzerland

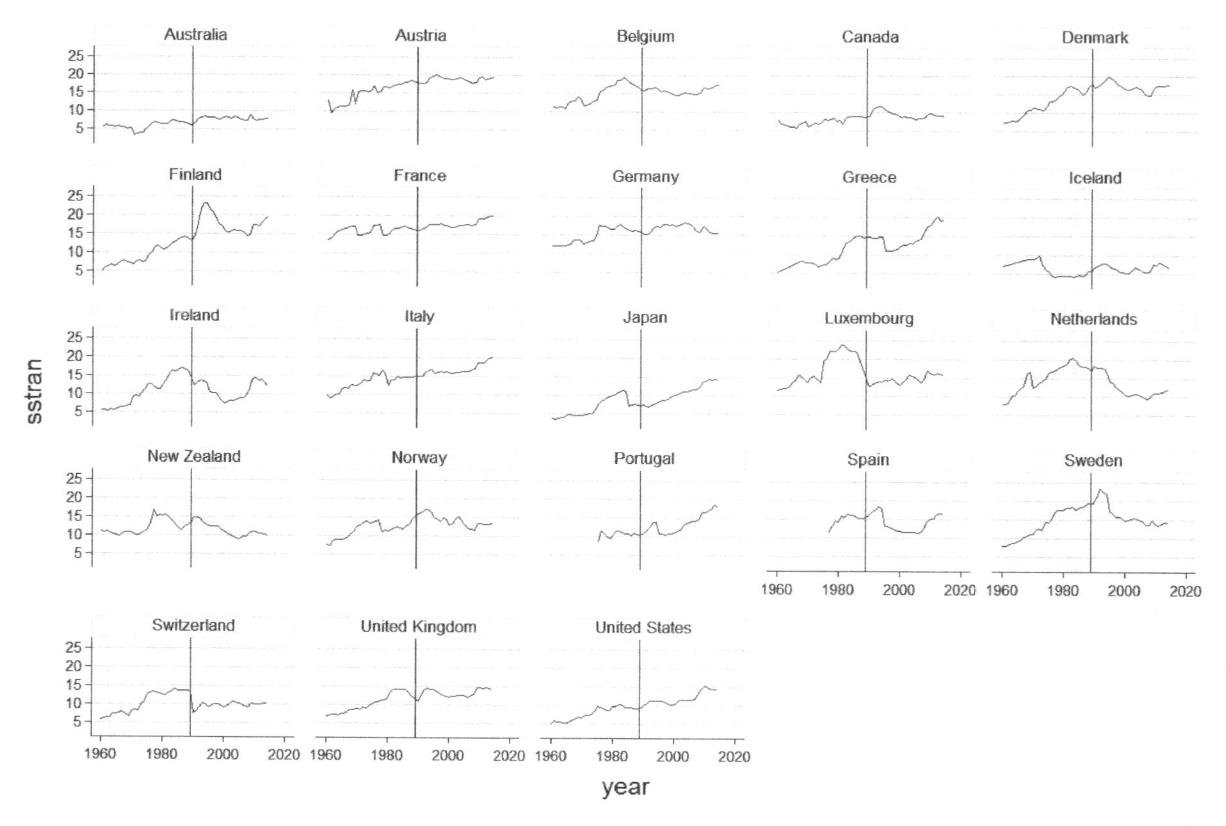

Figure 1. The trends of social security transfers as a percentage of GDP in different countries.

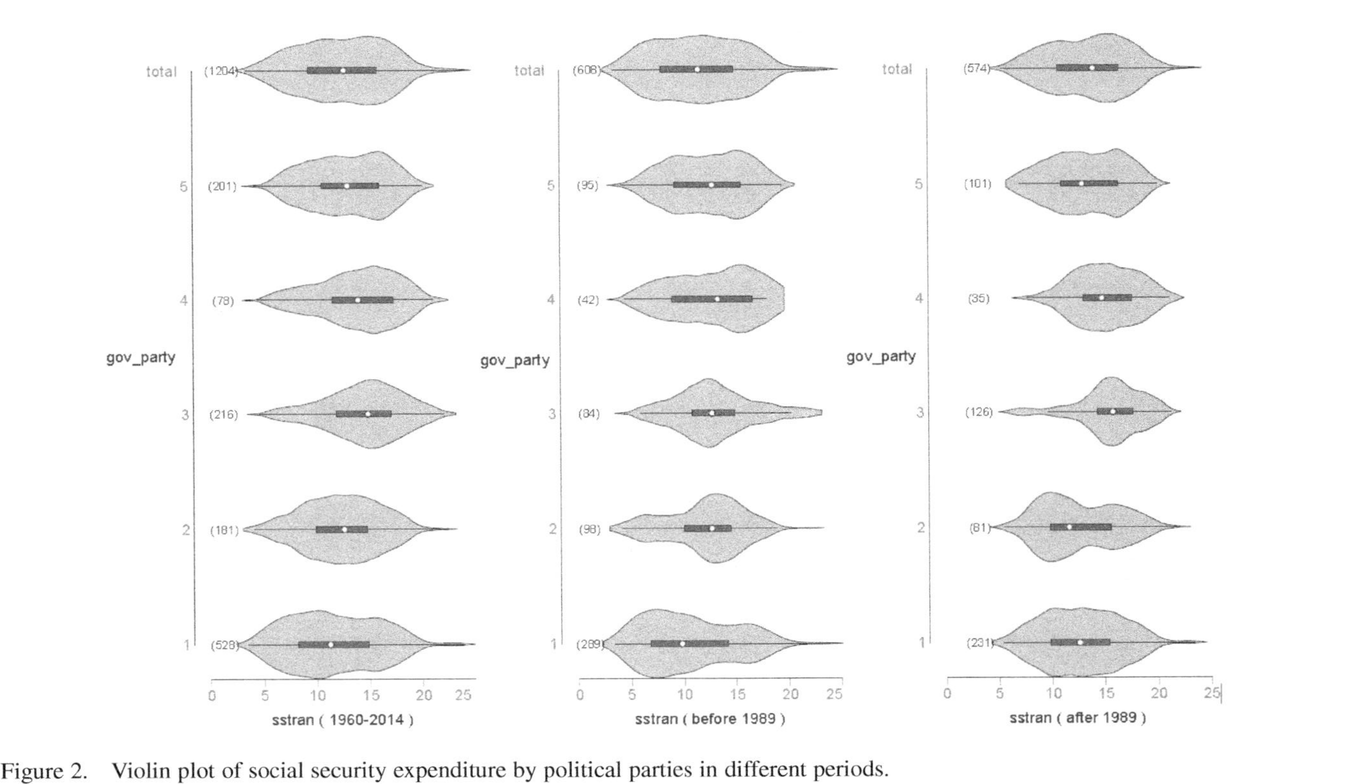

Figure 2. Violin plot of social security expenditure by political parties in different periods.

Note: In each violin plot, the white point is a marker for the median of the data; the small dark gray boxes indicate the interquartile range (between 25th and 75th percentiles) and the thin black line denotes the lower adjacent value to the upper adjacent value. The shaded area depicts a density trace, plotted symmetrically above and below the horizontal box plot. Beside the violin plot, the value in parentheses denotes the number of observations in a specific party.

fluctuated wildly in and around 1976, which might be caused by the OPEC oil crisis that occurred at that time. In addition, social security expenditures in all countries clearly changed around 1989. The reason, in our opinion, is that the revolutions of 1989 led to the end of the Cold War and the alteration of the political and economic systems of the socialist countries in Eastern Europe, as well as to further changes in politics around the rest of the world.

We then present individual violin plots in Figure 2, allowing for comparisons within each ideology and greater understanding of the social security expenditure distributions under different periods. As can be seen from Figure 2, social security expenditure increases significantly after 1989 in almost all of the ideology categories, for which the violin plots move to the right. In addition, the distributions under political parties have undergone great changes since 1989. One striking feature is that the right-wing exhibits substantial skewness before 1989, with the tail extending well to the left, which fully indicates that a majority of right wing ideologies stand for large social security expenditure. In contrast, the situation changed after 1989, and another wing appears to be in a normal distribution. Therefore, it is imperative to examine the relationship between ideology and social security expenditure under different historical periods.

With the year 1989 being the necessary demarcation point, the authors provide a dynamic interpretation of the changes in modern political parties, by analyzing the effect of big events on political parties and by comparing the differences in the impact of political parties on social security policies during different time periods.

4. The Empirical Analysis Results

Other than the pooled ordinary least square (OLS), there remain two models that are specifically applicable to analyze the panel data, namely, fixed effects and random effects. Since the choice of the model greatly affects the result of this analysis, we first employ an F-Test to investigate whether the individual effect is significant and compare the fixed effects model as well as the Pooled OLS. Second, the Breusch–Pagan Lagrange Multiplier (LM) Test is used to make a decision between the random effects model and the OLS model. Then the Hausman Test is utilized to determine the proper model when faced with fixed effects versus random effects. And finally, these tests suggest in this chapter that the fixed effects model is more appropriate.

Considering that the fixed effects model might be heteroskedastic, autocorrelated, and cross-sectionally dependent, it is better to use Driscoll–Kraay Standard Errors to estimate the results. (Driscoll & Kraay, 1998; Garmann, 2014; Hoechle, 2007) Therefore, we use the procedure of *xtscc* in stata to obtain a fixed-effects regression with Driscoll–Kraay standard errors, which are heteroscedasticity consistent and robust to the very general forms of cross-sectional and temporal dependence when the time dimension is large.

With the F-test, LM test and Hausman test, the fixed effects model is finally chosen to analyze the data obtained from 23 countries. In addition, the results of the fixed effects model are more vividly reported in Table 3 via data visualization instead of traditional tables.

Model A in Table 3 shows that right-wing and extreme right-wing parties have a significantly positive effect on social security expenditure, but the coefficients of the left-wing and extreme left-wing parties are non-significant. Extant studies have concluded that left-wing parties are more likely to increase social security expenditure than their right-wing counterparts, but the conclusion of this chapter challenges the traditional perception. The estimates indicate that, at least in some developed democracies — the research subjects of this chapter — left-wing parties do not substantially raise social security transfers as a percentage of GDP. Therefore, Hypothesis 1 is validated.

The revolutions of 1989 resulted in the situation whereby the opposition between left-wing and right-wing parties in all countries was precipitously reduced and the policy differences of ideological parties were gradually narrowed. Recent studies have pointed out that, after the Cold War, major developed countries ended ideological conflicts as well as the arm race and gave more expenditure to improve people's living standard (Dixon & John, 1992; Giddens, 1999). Model B in Table 3 shows that after 1989, both left-wing and right-wing parties have little effect on social security expenditure, but Model C in Table 3 indicates that before

Table 3. The estimates of the fixed effects model based on the panel data of 23 countries.

Variable	Model A 1960–2014	Model B after 1989	Model C before 1989
party_1	0.356*	0.198	0.16
	(2.09)	(0.95)	(0.82)
party_2	0.753***	0.325	0.560***
	(3.94)	(1.34)	(2.91)
party_4	−0.00299	−0.101	0.205
	(−0.01)	(−0.32)	(0.95)
party_5	−0.204	−0.104	−0.494
	(−0.88)	(−0.39)	(−1.54)
Net union membership, in thousands	−0.000218*	−0.000685***	0.000494***
	(−1.57)	(−5.63)	(4.84)
Growth of real GDP	−0.168***	−0.207***	−0.0385*
	(−6.17)	(−6.19)	(−1.74)
Unemployment rate	0.327***	0.372***	0.316***
	(8.29)	(7.50)	(14.49)
Total receipts (revenue) of general government	0.249***	0.260***	0.199***
	(10.53)	(7.68)	(5.36)
Total labor force	−0.0874**	−0.0106	0.0109
	(−2.68)	(−0.36)	−0.39
Constant	4.202	4.723*	0.436
	(1.62)	(1.78)	(0.30)
Country fixed effects	Yes	Yes	Yes
Year fixed effects	Yes	Yes	Yes
N	955	503	431
F	14097.3	534.3	2360.8

Notes: Robust standard errors are in parentheses; *, **, and *** denotes significance levels of 1%, 0.5%, and 0.1%, respectively.

1989, right-wing parties played a crucial positive role in social security expenditure. This conclusion says a lot for the fact that it is unrealistic for voters to try to change the welfare system by voting, because the impact of ideological parties on social security policies is unavoidably fading with the current development of party politics. In this way, Hypothesis 2 is confirmed.

The authors find that other factors, including government revenues, unemployment, labor force, and GDP growth rate, also make a substantial contribution to social security expenditure, which is consistent with the conclusion in the existing researches. (Gersovitz & Paxson, 1996; Kitao, 2014; Lusinyan & Thornton, 2012; Narayan & Narayan, 2006; Rickne, 2013; Shelton, 2007).

5. Robustness Test

We performed the robustness test to examine the reliability of the results obtained in our study. First, the data of 35 countries in this chapter were acquired from the CPDS; while the comprehensive analysis above was based on the data of only 23 countries, since 12 countries with more than 15% of missing data were artificially deleted. To further examine our above results, the robustness test was conducted with the data of 35 countries, including the data of the 12 deleted countries. The regression results of the fixed effects model are presented in Table 4, and the list of countries is provided in Table A.2.

As can be seen from Table 4, from 1960 to 2014, right-wing and extreme right-wing parties positively affect social security expenditure, but the impact of left-wing parties and extreme left-wing parties is non-significant. Before 1989, right-wing parties have an enormous implication for social security expenditure. While after 1989, the impact of left-wing and right-wing parties is of little significance. In addition, the estimates of other control variables are in line with the above conclusion that we draw. This confirms that our aforementioned conclusion is reliable.

Second, in the above dummy variables, political parties are divided into five types according to their ideologies, which is conducive to the improvement of the model's accuracy, but limits the sample number for each type of variable, especially when the differences between ideological parties of all countries started narrowing after 1989. To test whether the size of each type of variables affects the results, we performed the

Table 4. The estimates of the fixed effects model based on the panel data of 35 countries.

Variable	1960–2014	After 1989	Before 1989
party_1	0.271 (1.74)*	0.00516 (0.31)	0.16 (0.82)
party_2	0.501 (3.33)***	0.0529 (0.32)	0.560 (2.91)***
party_4	0.159 (1.05)	0.174 (1.05)	0.205 (0.95)
party_5	−0.227 (−1.14)	−0.261 (−1.53)	−0.494 (−1.54)
Net union membership, in thousands	−0.000205 (−1.51)*	−0.000686 (−5.19)***	0.000494 (−4.84)***
Growth of real GDP	−0.153 (−7.59)***	−0.163 (−6.66)***	−0.0385 (−1.74)
Unemployment rate	0.304 (9.3)***	0.314 (8.52)***	0.316 (14.49)***
Total receipts (revenue) of general government	0.249 (10.88)***	0.236 (7.46)***	0.199 (5.36)***
Total labor force	−0.0839 (−2.59)***	−0.00762 (−0.24)	−0.0109 (−0.39)
Constant	3.981 (1.54)	1.588 (0.65)	−2.237 (−1.44)
Country fixed effects	Yes	Yes	Yes
Year fixed effects	Yes	Yes	Yes
N	1116	664	431
F	34670.8	50533.6	273416.3

Notes: Robust standard errors are in parentheses; *, **, and *** denotes significance levels of 1%, 0.5%, and 0.1%, respectively.

robustness test by classifying ideological parties into three types, i.e., right-wing, center and left-wing parties, which contributes to increasing the size of each type of variables and improving the reliability of the regression results. The specifically created dummy variables are as follows:

$$\text{party}0_1 = \begin{cases} 1, & \text{if right-wing} \\ 0, & \text{if not right-wing} \end{cases} \qquad \text{party}0_3 = \begin{cases} 1, & \text{if left-wing} \\ 0, & \text{if not left-wing} \end{cases}$$

$$\text{party}0_2 = \begin{cases} 1, & \text{if center} \\ 0, & \text{if not center} \end{cases}$$

Table 5 shows that the impact of right-wing parties on social security expenditure is positive but that of left-wing parties is non-significant. It also demonstrates that, after 1989, both left-wing and right-wing parties do not much affect social security expenditure. While

Table 5. The estimates of the fixed effects model with three types of parties.

Variable	1960–2014	After 1989	Before 1989
party_1	0.481 (3.03)***	0.233 (1.18)	0.333 (1.84)*
party_3	−0.0834 (−0.45)	−0.0851 (−0.35)	−0.127 (−0.53)
Net union membership	−0.000215 (−1.52)	−0.000685 (−5.68)***	0.000482 (4.59)***
Growth of real GDP	−0.173 (−6.46)***	−0.209 (−6.19)***	−0.0461 (−2.09)**
Unemployment rate	0.326 (8.49)***	0.372 (7.31)***	0.307 (14.09)***
Total receipts (revenue) of general government	0.248 (10.43)***	0.258 (7.54)***	0.200 (5.31)***
Total labor force	−0.0874 (−2.73)**	−0.0106 (−0.36)	−0.0226 (−0.83)
Constant	4.15 (1.64)	0.817 (0.32)	−1.576 (−1.09)
Country fixed effects	Yes	Yes	Yes
Year fixed effects	Yes	Yes	Yes
N	955	503	431
F	15123.5	80888.5	451370125.9

Notes: Robust standard errors are in parentheses; *, **, and *** denotes significance levels of 1%, 0.5%, and 0.1%, respectively.

before 1989, the impact of right-wing parties is significant. And the estimates of other control variables are in conformity with the earlier-stated conclusion in this chapter. Therefore, these conclusions are validated to be robust.

6. Conclusion and Discussion

Although extensive previous studies have shown that left-wing parties are more willing to support the development of social welfare. And after carefully analyzing the data of nine welfare states from 1972 to 1990s, Huber and Stephens (2001) argued that left-wing parties have a significant positive correlation with social welfare expenditure in welfare states. However, the traditional theory of party politics cannot explain why right-wing parties in Western Europe have won successive electoral successes in the past 20 years when welfare states have largely reduced social welfare expenditure and civilians have continually pursued social benefits (Arzheimer & Carter, 2006).

The results of this chapter demonstrated that ideologies of parties indeed impact on social security expenditure, while they also indicated that left-wing parties in democracies are not so inclined to increase social security expenditure as assumed by the traditional perception. In our opinion, four factors are capable of explaining this situation. The first is that there are less left-wing parties in power in democracies compared with right-wing parties. The second is that right-wing parties have to meet the demands of voters increasingly in order to win elections, with more expenditure on social security being part of the necessary response.

The third is that, the limited number of research subjects inevitably causes traditional studies to argue that left-wing parties devote themselves to increasing social welfare. Existing studies listed in this chapter only take a single country or several European countries (less than 10 countries) as research subject(s), and on this basis, they firmly insisted that left-wing parties tend to spend more on social welfare. However, our findings overturn these traditional viewpoints via examining much more data and countries (Bingham Powell Jr, 2009). The fourth is that the differences between left-wing parties and right-wing parties in ideologies and policy preferences are narrowing, which means, to win the support of swing voters, the party identification of different parties becomes more blurred and the ideological distance between candidates gets increasingly closer. (Inglehart & Klingemann, 1976; Kitschelt & Wilkinson, 2007).

The systematic and comprehensive analysis provided by this chapter tested and supported the "ideology matters" hypothesis, however, this study also indicated that the impact of parties' ideologies on different countries changes in different historical periods (for example, the before and after revolutions of 1989). This finding reminds voters of considering their choice carefully when they are voting for a party turnover. Besides, it also provides voters with a new reference point when they are making their voting decisions. Nevertheless, the traditional cognition of party preferences does not necessarily apply to the current situation, especially around social policy.

Certainly, there are some areas where this chapter has to make further improvements. In the first place, after studying Japanese election, Estévez-Abe (2008) argued that the electoral rules often determine the policy choices of political parties. Likewise, some scholars claimed that culture is an essential element in the outputs of social security policies. (Vivekanandan & Kurian, 2005) Taylor-Gooby (2002) also pointed out that culture is of great importance to the outputs of social policies, and the culture framework, which is related to the national value, the market and the concept of family welfare, necessarily sets an impact on the policy structure (Taylor-Gooby, 2002). These existing findings suggest that, in different cultural contexts and political systems (including institutions, party systems, and electoral rules), parties with the same ideological label may possibly make different choices. However, this chapter did not analyze the factors that have something to do with cultural contexts and political systems, because there are difficulties in controlling these factors in large-N macro comparisons and there are limits in the available statistical methods. In the second place, we did not explore the impact of the center parties on social security policies for the reason that the median party (a variable) is deleted in this study to avoid the dummy variable trap and multicollinearity. In the third place, future researches should further test the impact of ideological parties on high welfare states and low welfare states. Besides, the universal potential implications and reference values of our conclusions need to be tested in more countries, because the research subjects in this chapter are mainly developed democracies.

All in all, there are many factors which can influence social policy, such as interest group activity, context and culture. And after studying the impact of party ideology on social policy, this article enriches our understandings of the factors that induce and shape the process of social policy in democracies.

Appendix A

Table A.1. The list of 23 countries.

Country	Country
Australia	Austria
Belgium	Canada
Denmark	France
Finland	Greece
Germany	Italy
Iceland	Luxembourg
Ireland	Norway
Japan	Spain
Netherlands	United Kingdom
New Zealand	Switzerland
Portugal	United States
Sweden	

Table A.2. The list of 35 countries.

Australia	Cyprus	France	Ireland	Luxembourg	Poland	Spain
Austria	Czech Republic	Germany	Italy	Malta	Portugal	Sweden
Belgium	United States	Greece	Japan	Netherlands	Romania	Switzerland
Canada	New Zealand	Hungary	Latvia	Estonia	Slovakia	Finland
Croatia	United Kingdom	Iceland	Lithuania	Norway	Slovenia	Denmark

Chapter 4

Strikes of Workers and Ideological Turnover in Democracies: A Panel Vector Auto-regression Approach*

We performed a panel vector auto-regression model to analyze the generally ignored relationship between workers' strikes and ideological turnover. Based on the panel data of 20 developed democracies in the period from 1960 to 2014, the chapter finds that the activity level of strikes affects ideological turnover with lags, and the effect is not significant in the first year. Conversely, ideological turnover has no significant current or lagged effect on strikes. We also evaluate the social costs of strikes. These results have been confirmed as reliable by the robustness test.

1. Introduction

2016 Presidential Election witnessed political party turnover and protests in the US. Despite of that, the memory about various social movements happened during the Obama administration is still fresh, such as the far-reaching Occupy Wall Street movement, which, to a certain extent, have

*I am indebted to Luyue Xie, for remarkable research assistance.

had a significant impact on politics. Just like in 2008 when Obama, the Democratic candidate, defeated John McCain, the Republican candidate, in 2016, social movements including strikes, protests, assemblies, and even work stoppages, broke out against Donald Trump, the Republican candidate, after he won the most recent election. US gender equality activists were even preparing for a nationwide strike when women would walk out of work and protest against the election of Donald Trump. In fact, information from the Bureau of Labor Statistics indicates that the numbers of work stoppages involving 1,000 or more workers, and strike activities, always increase around the time of presidential elections. Similar situations also occurs in other advanced democracies.

In this chapter, we conduct research to figure out whether strikes that appeared within the administration of one party would impact on the re-election of that party and result in party turnover or ideological turnover. Meanwhile, this research will also try to answer the question that whether party turnover or ideological turnover, in turn, would bring about a new round of strikes after a certain period of time. Some scholars have already focused on this topic. For example, in *States, Parties, and Social Movements,* Goldstone observed that a link between party politics and social movements, including strikes, has appeared in the US and the rest of the world since the 1950s. Goldstone (2003) also argued that the study of strikes and the study of political parties, which in fact are closely related, are generally believed by scholars to be absolutely irrelevant and entirely separated. However, the two study fields are closely related and strikes, which often impact on election campaigns and party policy preferences, can even result in party turnover.

The earliest research studying the relationship between strikes and political turnover can be traced back to 1906. Luxemburg (1906) pointed out that strikes are often seen as a significant component of the outbreak of revolution and of regime change. For instance, a strike of Moscow workers was closely linked with the Russian Revolution of 1917 (Koenker, 1981). And after the establishment of modern states, strikes around the world have still been emerging wave after wave, because people want, not only to obtain all kinds of rights, including civic rights, political rights, and social rights, but also to express their opinions on international policies and treaties (Lambert, 2005; Rees, 1985). With the development and improvement of democratic systems, regular elections in developed democracies have been attested to be the main trigger for government turnover. However, strikes can still easily become important during election process. In this context, strikes are often regarded as an important variable that can have a subtle influence on election outcomes through affecting voter behaviors, and political attitudes (Ng, 1991; Weakliem, 1993). In other words, the political activities of parties provide motivation, opportunities and possibilities for strikes and also impact on the successes and the failures of election campaigns.

In many countries, the democratic electoral system *per se* comes about because of strikes. Therefore, we cannot thoroughly understand the political processes in most western democracies if we ignored the close relationship between party politics and strikes. Nevertheless, up to now, studies have not attached great attention to the bidirectional relationship between strikes and government turnover (party turnover). In addition, they have not systematically analyzed whether strikes are in a reciprocal causation with party turnover or whether the reciprocal causation presents in the time dimension.

This chapter innovatively applies a panel vector auto-regression approach (PVAR) to political science and carefully analyzes the panel data of 20 developed democracies in the period from 1960 to 2014. All variables in a VAR enter the model in the same way: each variable has an equation explaining its evolution based on its own lagged values, the lagged values of the other variables in the model, and an error term. Nevertheless, VAR modeling does not also require as much knowledge about the forces influencing a variable as structural models do with simultaneous equations. Our findings show that only a one-way causal relationship exists between strikes and ideological turnover, that is, strikes have a significant impact on ideological turnover, but there is no reciprocal effect. We also assess the average number of working days lost as a result of strike activity and the indirect social cost resulting from ideological turnover. Besides, our research provides a theoretical basis for predictions about election outcomes and party turnover in democracies.

The other parts of our research are organized as follows. The second part is the relevant literature review. In the third part, the variables and data descriptions are presented. Finally, we discuss the results and potential implications of this study.

2. Strike and Government Turnover

To present the analysis of our research clearly, we will define our key concepts and measurement indexes of strikes before further reviewing the relevant research literature. First, we classify government turnover as leadership turnover (or a change in rulers) and ideological turnover (or a change in the rulers' ideology) in a way that other scholars use in their studies (Milanovic, Hoff, & Horowitz, 2010). Second, strikes are purposeful entities in which people are organized to strive for a common goal. This chapter weighs the strike index by measuring the number of strikes in different countries based on available data.

Firstly, existing studies have paid attention to the types of strikes, classifying them as student strikes, worker strikes, and public sector strikes. In the early 20th century, student strikes tended to occur at the starting point of a revolution, and this is particularly apparent in communist countries (Flacks, 1970; Habermas, 1971; Wasserstrom, 1991). For instance, the Communist Party, in the early days, played its own roles by promoting student strikes and worker strikes. Since the middle and late 20th century, students may meet their demands (such as reducing tuition fees) by striking when some particular political opportunity arises (Jenkins, Jacobs, & Agnone, 2003). At the same time, however, their strikes may be forcibly suppressed by the government (Perry, 2007; Rhoads & Mina, 2001), such as the student protest in Tiananmen Square in 1989 (Walder, 1991). The social influences of worker strikes and public sector strikes are such that they are not only related to the daily life of each citizen, but also concerned with the stability of the social order (Mattoni, 2016).

Secondly, regarding to the factors which have an impact on the emergence of strikes, researchers have also summarized that there are two main streams of quantitative researches on the determinants of aggregate strike activity over time and across countries: the economic approach and the organizational/political approach (Franzosi, 1989). Economists have demonstrated that strike activity is linked to the business cycle (Campolieti,

Hebdon, & Dachis, 2014; Devereux & Hart, 2011), and sociologists along with political scientists have shown that it is linked in the longer term to the organizational capacities of the workers and to their political position in national power structures (Amenta & Zylan, 1991; McAdam, McCarthy, & Zald, 1996). Although the political, economic, and social factors that led to strikes have already been analyzed in existing studies, research concerning how a change in government leadership can affect strikes remains limited.

Thirdly, the spillover effect of strikes has also attracted the attention of academic research. On the one hand, the demands of workers' strikes, such as improving individual rights, increasing income, changing leadership of the labor organization, maintaining sustainable development, and protecting the environment, may be largely satisfied. On the other hand, Downs (1957) indicated that each political behavior has its own social and economic costs. Although strikes in modern democracies rarely require the replacement of leaders, the question still exists as to whether strikes will affect the political attitude held by a coalition of supporters in the re-election of leaders, and how this would affect the votes for each political candidate. In other words, we would like to clarify whether strikes have an impact on leadership transitions and are wasteful of the social resources.

In recent years, a few publications have applied insights from strikes to government turnover. This body of work has focused on analyzing the factors that result in strikes as well as party turnover, and has examined spillover effects of the two.

In the first place, strikes do impact on government succession. In the preliminary stage of capitalist countries, radical social movements, such as workers' strikes, were essential reasons for institutional transfer and regime change. The combination of economic development, the establishment of social welfare systems and the improvement in the protections of workers' rights has reduced the number of radical social movements for regime subversion and has also moderated other social movements. However, Blumer (1995) and Tilly and Tarrow (2006) have stated that current social movements could still solve specific social issues or promote the establishment of relevant systems. For example, the two financial crises in the late 20th and early 21st century have caused a succession of workers' strikes from North America to Europe, with the workers' enthusiasm for strikes being consistently strong. Strikes, including wildcat strikes and organized ones, are representative of social movements. Numerous studies on the effect of social movements deal explicitly with public policy and some argue that the potential power of everyday people is a deciding force in a nation's political process (Piven, 2006).

In the second place, strikes may have an impact on party turnover. They will exacerbate tensions between the ruling parties and the opposition parties, which further changes the current political balance or causes national elections to be held sooner or to be postponed. Taking America as an example, since the 1960s, strikes have had a powerful effect in reshaping American politics. Vanden (2007) has stressed that strikes in Latin American countries could possibly give rise to political transformations.

In summary, recent studies have focused their attention on analyzing the impact of strikes on the transition from authoritarian states to democracies. However, in western democracies, with their sound political structures and regular national elections, incumbents voluntarily leave office after losing at the polls (Knutsen & Wig, 2015). Meanwhile, it is obvious that these studies mainly analyze the impact of strikes on policy makers instead of party turnover, not to mention ideological turnover. This means that the impact of strikes on party turnover in regular elections in modern democracies has yet to be studied thoroughly. Recent studies have consistently applied quantitative research methods, which do not measure the impact of strikes on ideological turnover from a time dimension. However, Pierson (2011) stated that research on a social phenomenon should attach importance to the timing and duration of its impact. Studies on social memory have pointed out that collective memory or public memory of public events fades with time and that the impact of public events weakens with the fading of memory (Jeffrey & Robbins, 1998). In consideration of the previous scholarship and time dimension, we put forward the following hypothesis.

Hypothesis 1: Ceteris paribus, the growth of strikes has a significant current or lagged effect on ideological turnover.

In addition to the fact that the new government may not have encompassed control over the economy, new leadership may or may not promote pro-growth policies, and some new leaders may have redistribution and social welfare policies that are not directly linked to overall economic growth. Londregan and Poole (1990), Alesina and Perotti (1996) all argued that the possible impact of turnover on economic performance has been incorporated into cross-country empirical work on growth and investment through the inclusion of measures of political instability. Other scholars working on the economic consequences of political connections have examined the differential impact of political turnover on politically connected firms (Ferguson & Voth, 2008), based on the panel data consisting of 80 countries and 5 years.

Using a dynamic political economy model with two political parties alternating in office, Elgin (2010) found that different political parties tend to put into effect different policies for taxation and social welfare. Based on the data from 1985 to 2006, in OECD countries, he also discovered that the political instability among different ideological governments influences the level of labor market institutions and taxes (Lucifora & Moriconi, 2015). Although these existing studies have followed the effect on social policies as well as on social welfare systems brought about by the rotation of different parties, as yet, there has not been an in-depth exploration into whether the rotation of different parties would directly or indirectly affect strikes. In particular, in the context in which different ideological parties take turns in power, the problem about "what impacts do the ideological differences have on strikes?" has yet to be addressed. Lucifora and Moriconi (2015) assumed that there are two parties in the political arena. However, they have not shown clearly whether the ideologies between these two political parties are consistent with each other.

Does ideological turnover have an impact on social movements? The importance of ideology is further highlighted in the wide range of empirical research that shows how ideological structures affect individual behaviors (Carmines & D'Amico, 2014). Douglass Cecil North (1990) also put forward an idea that different institutions have major impacts on social realities. However, few studies have explored policy changes resulting from party turnover under the democratic system. In fact, different parties in a democratic country may have various policy preferences, all impacting on the appearance and development of strikes.

For example, since his election, some of President Trump's remarks and policies have brought about contentious disputes and nationwide social movements along with strikes. On that basis, we propose the following hypothesis:

Hypothesis 2: Ceteris paribus, ideological turnover has a significant lagged effect on the growth of strikes.

3. Research Design

The majority of the data used in this study are from the Comparative Political Data Set (CPDS) (Armingeon, Isler, Knöpfel, Weisstanner, & Engler, 2016), which has been acknowledged as credible in academic circles (Layton-Henry, 2006; Lijphart, 2002). CPDS is a collection of political and institutional country-level data. Why did we choose CPDS as our core data set? To our knowledge, there are at least three databases containing leader turnover information, Cross-National Time-Series Data Archive (Banks & Wilson, 2013), Change in Source of Leader Support (CHISOLS) Dataset (Mattes, Leeds, & Matsumura, 2016), and Archigos: A Database on Political Leaders (Goemans *et al.*, 2009). Unlike the CPDS, these three datasets only provide information about when a leader change occurs but not code the direction of that change, especially the ideology of the leader.

Currently, the CPDS data are used in numerous studies that are published in various peer reviewed journals (Armingeon & Schädel, 2015; Obinger, Schmitt, & Zohlnhoefer, 2014). This dataset consists (mostly) of annual data for 35 democratic OECD and/or EU-member countries for the period 1960 to 2014. It is suited to cross-national, longitudinal and pooled time-series analyses. To ensure the quality of the data, 16 countries were omitted from our study because large portions of their data (15% or more for any category or year) were missing, so our final sample consists of the panel data of 20 developed democracies in the period from 1960 to 2014 (Table 1).

This chapter analyzes the bidirectional relationship between strikes and ideological turnover along with the social costs resulting from strikes. Taking the data availability and extant studies into consideration, we adopt the ideology turnover variable from the CPDS, i.e., new ideological

Table 1. Countries of analysis.

Australia	Italy
Austria	Japan
Belgium	Netherlands
Canada	New Zealand
Denmark	Norway
Finland	Spain
France	Sweden
Germany	Switzerland
Iceland	United Kingdom
Ireland	United States

composition of the cabinet (0: no change, 1: change). This calculation is based on the cabinet composition (Schmidt-Index) of the CPDS.

The strike index is measured by *strike*, i.e., the index of strike activity. Social cost is weighed by *wdlost*, i.e., working days lost (due to strikes and lockouts) per 1,000 workers. Large labor force differences between countries lead to a weak correlation between the index of strike activity and working days lost (the correlation coefficient is 0.4653, see Table A.1 in the Appendix for details). Therefore, it is appropriate to apply the variable *wdlost* in the model to observe social costs. These data are taken from the database of International Labor Office (ILO).

In addition, we also fully consider several standard political science variables that affect government turnover, such as the growth of GDP and receipts (total receipts of general government as a percentage of GDP). We collect these data from the World Bank.

Existing studies have demonstrated that the structural change in parliamentary seats is closely related to ideological turnover. For this reason, our paper adopts the variable total government support (seat share of all parties in government, weighted by the number of days in office in a given year), the calculation of which is primarily based on Schmidt and Beyer (1992).

We also consider the inflation rate and the unemployment rate in the robustness test, which collected from the AMECO (annual macroeconomic database of the European Commission) database. Table 2

Table 2. Variable descriptive statistics.

Variable	Definition	Mean	Max	Min	P50	P25	P75	Std. dev.	N
strike	Social movements (scaled by strike)	152.71	2841.49	0	41.75	6.34	171.71	275.6	1004
wdlost	Working days lost	2217.98	66413.8	0	233.62	33.05	1526.9	5725.47	1019
gov_sup	Total government support: seat share of all parties in government	56.22	95.2	0	54.32	49.68	61.4	12.12	1083
realgdpgr	Growth of real GDP	2.94	13.06	−8.27	2.93	1.5	4.44	2.65	1064
receipts	Total receipts (revenue) of general government as a percentage of GDP.	41.24	59.86	19.97	40.92	34.78	47.94	8.47	965
unemp	Unemployment rate	5.47	26.1	0	5.1	2.3	7.7	3.91	1083
inflation	Inflation rate	5.10	83.95	−4.48	3.295	1.945	6.335	6.21	1080

Table 3. Dummy variable descriptive statistics.

Variable	Definition		Percentage	Total
Gov_new	Ideological turnover	0: No change	77.91%	100%
		1: Change	22.09%	

Notes: Own calculations are primarily based on Manfred G Schmidt and Beyer (1992); from 1991 on, they are based on the political data published in the *European Journal of Political Research* (Political Data Yearbook, various issues). We classified parties as "left", "center", or "right" parties.

presents the variable descriptive statistics and Table 3 shows the dummy variable descriptive statistics.

4. Method: PVAR Model Estimation and Impulse Response Analysis

The PVAR model we applied here was put forward by scholars such as Holtz *et al.*, combining the traditional VAR approach, which treats all the variables in the system as endogenous, with the panel-data approach, which allows for unobserved individual heterogeneity (Holtz-Eakin, Newey, & Rosen, 1988). Although PVAR has been highly regarded by scholars in social science research (Brana, Djigbenou, & Prat, 2012; Lof & Malinen, 2014), it has not often been applied in the study of political science.

As with any panel approach, one advantage of panel VAR is that it allows for explicit inclusion of a fixed effect, which captures all time-invariant factors at a country level. The other advantage is that it takes the common time effects into consideration, capturing global factors that may affect the countries. This is important for our objectives as the inclusion of these fixed effects allows each country to have its own specific level of each of the factors in the model.

The main advantage of VAR system is that it captures the dynamic impact of the orthogonal shocks of one variable on another by virtue of impulse response functions when the other factors remain constant.

VAR is very useful in the case that the theoretical relationship of the variables has a weak foundation and the variables seem to be interactively determined.

However, a shortcoming of using the panel VAR system is the drastic decrease in the degrees of freedom, which allows for each variable to be added to the system (Griliches & Hausman, 1984). Consequently, we limit our system to five variables (six variables in the robustness test). In its general form, the five-variable PVAR model constructed in this chapter can be written as:

$$Z_{it} = \Pi_0 + \sum_{j=1}^{p} \Pi_{ij} Z_{it-j} + h_i + d_t + \varepsilon_{it}$$

where Z_{it} is a vector of five interested and key variables: *gov_new* (ideological turnover), *strike* (social movement), *wdlost* (working days lost), *realgdpr* (the growth of GDP), *receipts* (percentage of total receipts in GDP). Then $Z_{it} = (gov\_new_{it}\ strike_{it}\ wdlost_{it}\ realgdpr_{it}\ receipts_{it})^T$, $i = 1, 2, \ldots N$; $t = 1, 2, \ldots T$, in which N indicates the number of countries and T means the number of years. The h_i denotes the entity effect vector; and the d_t represents the time effect vector. All variables are defined in Tables 2 and 3.

Although various factors are involved in resulting in strikes and government change, we have also discovered that the growth of real GDP, and the total receipts (revenue) of general government as a percentage of GDP, are common factors. During a period of recession, problems such as falling incomes, rising unemployment rate and inflation are often presented. During a period of rapid economic growth, workers, with the support of their trade unions, will put more emphasis on the protection of their rights and interests (Bohlmann, Van Heerden, Dixon, & Rimmer, 2015). Therefore, no matter the real GDP grows or falls, strikes will usually act as a fuse in civil disturbance. At the same time, it will also make impact on the party turnover, and even on the ideological turnover in a country (Li & Zhou, 2005; Treisman, 2015).

The survival and behavior of leaders are often influenced by government revenue (De Mesquita & Smith, 2010). Current studies have also stated that the government revenues and the policy preferences of different political parties can exert an influence on each other (Gould, 2001). Moreover, fiscal revenue is the basis for the government to implement fiscal transfer and social welfare redistribution, which is particularly evident in developed welfare states (Strang & Chang, 1993). When government revenues are cut to the bone, several types of strikes will necessarily break out if the social income gap and social inequality cannot be managed effectively. Therefore, based on the analysis above, we will take into consideration in our models both variables, namely growth of real GDP and total receipts (revenue) of general government as a percentage of GDP.

In addition, the order of the variables matters to the results of impulse-response functions (Hamilton, 1994). In other words, the variables coming earlier in the system affect the following variables contemporaneously, while the later variables influence the previous ones only with a lag. We place ideological turnover and *strike* at the beginning because they are expected to affect other variables contemporaneously, while they may be impacted by other factors in the model with a lag. The growth of real GDP and *receipts* can respond to changes in ideological turnover as well as to *strikes*. But it will take more time to have an effect on ideological turnover. Thus, we adopt the order as is mentioned above: *gov_new, strike, wdlost, realgdpr, receipts*. However, the robustness of the ordering needs to be checked and we employ an alternate proper ordering of the variables in the robustness tests.

We use forward mean-differencing to eliminate the fixed effects that are correlated with the regressors due to lags in the dependent variables, and in this way we can avoid biased coefficients. Besides, we also use mean difference to eliminate the time effect. In this way, the orthogonality between transformed variables and lagged regressors is preserved, so we can use lagged regressors as instruments, and thus effectively estimate the coefficients by the generalized method of moments (GMM), a generic method for estimating parameters in statistical models. We employ the Love and Zicchino (2006) code for the panel VAR estimation in the econometric software STATA. Finally, based on the synthetic analysis of AIC along with BIC criteria and the convergence of the impulse response function, the PVAR model is selected with two lag intervals.

5. Empirical Results

5.1. *Time series stationarity test*

We conducted a stationary study on the data before the evaluation of the PVAR model in order to avoid a spurious regression and to ensure the stability of the PVAR model. The ideological turnover is a binary categorical variable, which is often regarded as a stationary series. The stability of other variables is examined via the Fisher-ADF (augmented Dickey–Fuller) and IPS (Im–Pesaran–Shin) Unit Root Test (Dickey & Fuller, 1979; Im, Pesaran, & Shin, 2003). The results suggest that except *receipts,* which is not confirmed, all the other variables significantly reject the null hypothesis of "presence of a unit root", indicating that they are stationary. The variable *government revenue* is found first difference stationary in the test which confirms that the time series is I (1). Since the premise of impulse response function is that all the variables are stationary, we employed the first difference of *government revenue* to avoid errors about the topics of interest. See Table A.2 for details about the results of the unit root test.

5.2. *PVAR model estimation*

The estimations of the PVAR model in Table 4 indicate that, in the model with *Strike* as the explained variable, the first-lagged index of strike activity has a positive coefficient with high significance, suggesting that the increase in the number of strikes has a self-reinforcing mechanism. In other words, the frequent occurrence of strikes without efficient solutions is likely to bring about a new round of strikes. The real GDP growth and government revenue growth have significant impacts on strikes with a lag or two, while the ideological turnover is not significant.

Table 4. The results of the panel VAR model estimation.

	Equations				
Variable	Strike	Ideological turnover	Working days lost	Real GDP	Receipts
Strike (t-1)	0.305	0.0001	−1.187	−0.0004	0.0001
	(3.91)***	(0.71)	(−1.99)**	(−0.72)	(0.4)
Ideological turnover (t-1)	29.049	0.238	212.840	0.105	0.251
	(1.18)	(5.09)***	(0.77)	(0.48)	(2.18)**
Working days lost (t-1)	0.004	0	0.590	0	0
	(1.2)	(−1.57)	(6.66)***	(1.28)	(−0.36)
Real GDP (t-1)	12.607	−0.004	113.535	0.567	0.069
	(2.82)***	(−0.5)	(2.36)**	(13.04)***	(3.72)***
Receipts (t-1)	−5.091	0.002	−100	−0.101	0.117
	(−0.56)	(0.15)	(−1.36)	(−1.34)	(2.64)***
Strike (t-2)	0.151	0.0002	−0.476	0.0006	0.0002
	(1.42)	(2.25)**	(−0.71)	(1.52)	(0.59)
Ideological turnover (t-2)	−7.026	−0.178	−220	0.513	0.035
	(−0.36)	(−4.62)***	(−1.06)	(2.33)**	(0.31)
Working days lost (t-2)	0.004	0	0.305	0	0
	(0.88)	(0.61)	(2.63)***	(−0.95)	(0.17)
Real GDP (t-2)	7.787	−0.013	102.960	0.063	0.027
	(1.76)*	(−1.87)*	(2.34)**	(1.41)	(1.38)
Receipts (t-2)	15.001	−0.0004	191.061	0.204	0.031
	(1.76)*	(−0.03)	(2.38)**	(3.06)***	(0.76)

Note: (a) *, **, *** indicate significance at the 1%, 0.5%, 0.1% level respectively. Standard errors are in parentheses. (b) t-1, t-2 mean first-order lag and second-order lag variables respectively.

In the model with ideological turnover as the explained variable, the coefficients of the first-lagged and two lagged intervals' ideological turnover are significant, indicating that the process of ideological turnover has a self-reinforcing mechanism, namely, one ideological turnover has a significant impact on the following ones. In addition, the coefficient of the first-lagged strike is small and non-significant, while the strike with a 2-year lag is significant at the 5% level. This suggests that the degree of strike activity has a positive impact on ideological turnover but the impact is lagged and non-significant in the first year. The ideology turnover does not exert a significant effect on *strike*. The conclusion here is consistent with what happens in the real world. Strikes seldom result in earlier presidential elections than planned in democracies with fixed election cycles, and large-scale strikes in a democratic country would not cause an immediate party turnover.

5.3. *Impulse response analysis*

The results of the PVAR model are further examined via the impulse response function which is conducive to presenting the impact of the exogenous shock of one variable on another. Ceteris paribus, we analyze the dynamic effect track and dynamic transmission mechanism of the shock of one variable on another, finding that the effect is unidirectional and pure.

Figure 1 describes the dynamic relationship between ideological turnover, the activity degree of strikes, working days lost, real GDP growth and government revenue growth, where the horizontal axis represents the number of lagged years (unit: year), the vertical axis is the response value of variables to shocks, the center line indicates the impulse response curve and the lines above and below it show the estimates of the 95% and 5% quantiles to reflect the estimation error range respectively.

We discuss general results first before focusing on the topics of our particular interests. Regarding to the dynamic relationship between ideological turnover and real GDP growth, the first column of the fourth row in Figure 1 indicates that one current ideological turnover leads to a

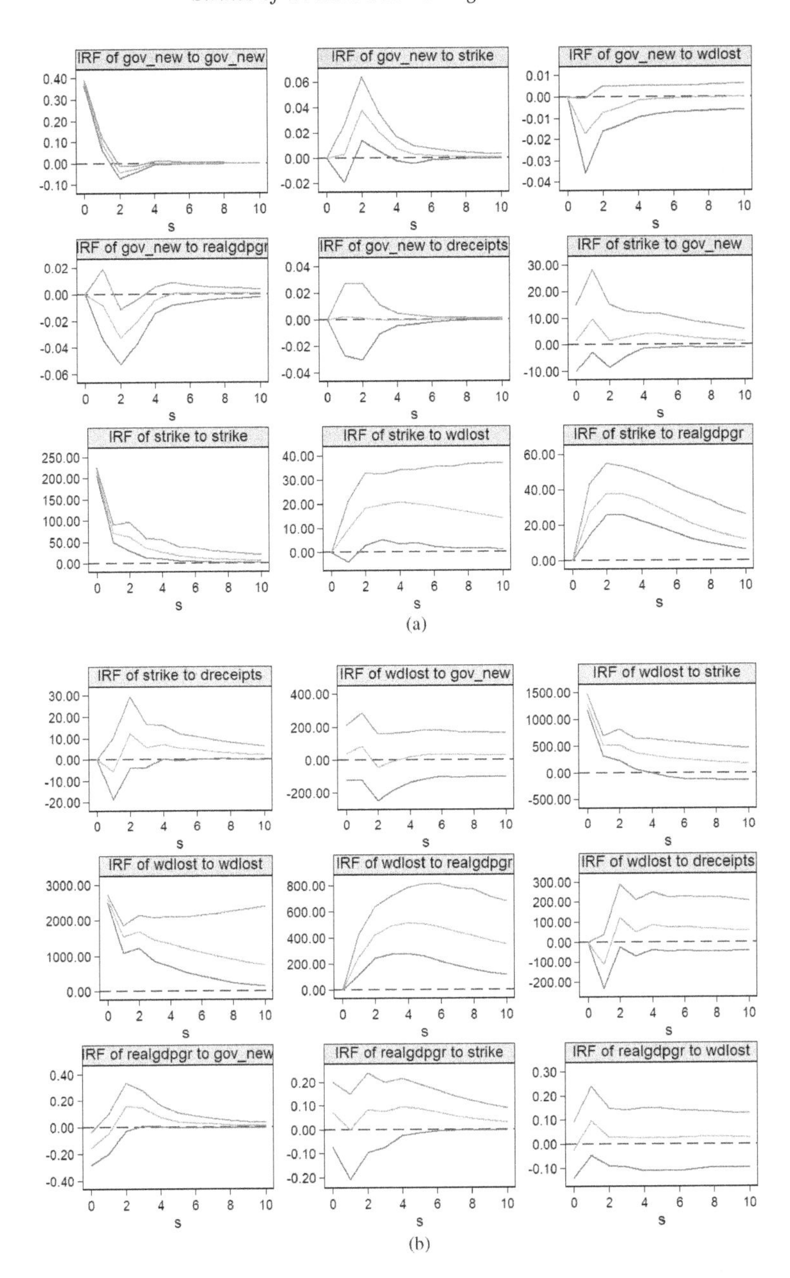

Figure 1. Impulse responses for 2 lag VAR of *gov_new, strike, wdlost, real GDP, receipts* (generated by Monte-Carlo with 200 reps).

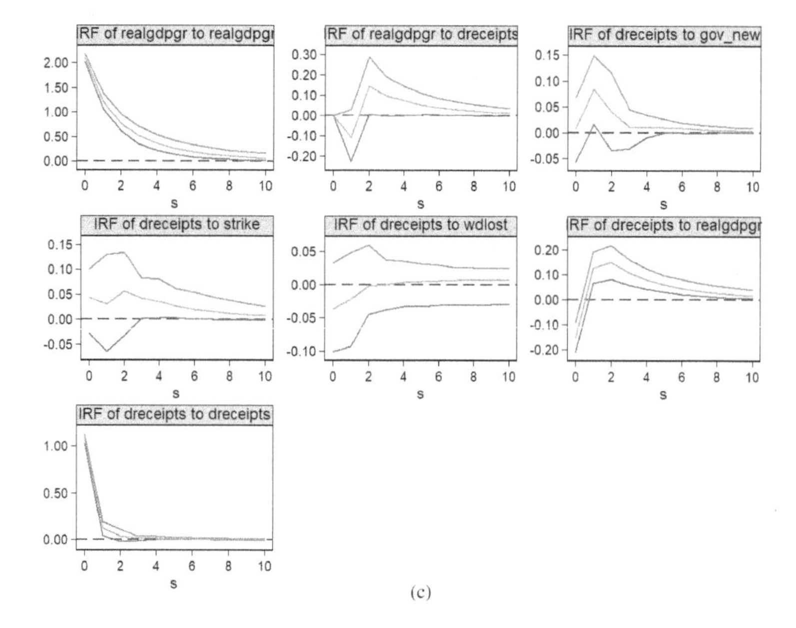

(c)

Figure 1. *(Continued)*

positive increase of real GDP growth in the second year, but the effect will then fade and disappear in the fourth year. We also note that, in response to a positive shock to the real GDP growth, the impact on ideological turnover is negative with a lag of 2–3 years. This implies that if the current ideological turnover makes a great contribution to the GDP, the ideology is likely to remain unchanged in the second and third years.

The first row of Figure 1 displays the impulse response of the ideological turnover to a one-standard-deviation shock towards other variables. The result presented in the first line of the second column shows that the impact of a positive shock on strikes and ideological turnover increases significantly with a lag of 2–3 years, while the impact disappears and becomes insignificant after the fourth year.

The impact of behavior on society often exhibits "hysteresis" (Abrahamson, 1997; Midtbø, 1999), which means that the growth of strikes has lagged effects on ideological turnover over a short term.

Thus, similarly, the political impact brought about by strikes cannot be revealed immediately.

The second row of Figure 1 describes the impulse response of strikes to a one-standard-deviation shock towards other variables. The left one shows our main result: in response to a positive shock towards the ideological turnover, the impact on social movements is not significant, which is consistent with our estimation. The response of the social movements to real GDP growth is fairly significant and the response approach is zero over time.

In addition, the chapter finds that, in response to a shock towards social movements, in general, working days lost firstly increase by 1,500 days, then sharply decline, and lastly gradually stabilize. Therefore, the social costs caused by social movements increases significantly in the first three years.

Meanwhile, we have noticed a shock from ideological turnover, which had remarkably influenced GDP growth during the second to the fourth year. GDP growth, which can, evidently, further affect working days lost, would also make impact on strikes. Thus, even if ideological turnover does not have an intuitively significant impact on social costs in statistical terms, it does influence working days lost indirectly by the following two means: ideological turnover→GDP growth→working days lost and ideological turnover→GDP growth→social movement→working days lost.

6. Robustness Test

We performed the following robustness tests to ensure the reliability and robustness of the results obtained in this chapter.

6.1. *Robustness test 1*

The seat distribution of parliamentary parties is directly related to ideological turnover. A government may be terminated at any time before the expiration of its parliamentary term if it loses the confidence of the parliament (Diermeier, Eraslan, & Merlo, 2002). Therefore, the government support is used to represent the parliamentary seat distribution in CPDS. This chapter also introduces the government support into the PVAR model and the results are as follows.

It can be seen from Figure 2 that, in response to a positive shock towards ideological turnover, the number of strikes shows no significant change. In addition, in response to a positive shock towards strike numbers, ideological turnover has increased significantly in the second and third years but has become stable after the fourth year, indicating that strikes can have hysteresis effects on ideological turnover. In response to a shock of the 1 unit standard deviation towards the number of strikes, working days lost have increased by 1,500,000 in general, but have declined sharply and disappeared in the fourth year. These conclusions are consistent with those of our study mentioned above. This shows that the model is robust and the results are explanatory.

Another interesting finding is the relationship between the government support and strikes. Though the shock of ideological turnover has no significant impact on strikes, the impulse response of strikes to a one-standard-deviation shock in government support clearly shows a positive impact, especially in the second and third years (in the third row and second column of Figure 2).

6.2. *Robustness test 2*

As the results of the impulse response are sensitive to the order of variables, in order to ensure the robustness of our findings, we estimated the panel VAR model with an alternate ordering of the variables and analyzed the impulse response results separately. Specifically, considering that except for strikes, fiscal policies and receipts may also exert an influence on ideological turnover, we change the ordering of variables in our basic model into: *gov_new, dreceipts, wdlost, strike, realgdpr.* To ensure that the ordering we imposed in the main model has no effect on our findings, we also test the model in which the variables are in a specific causal

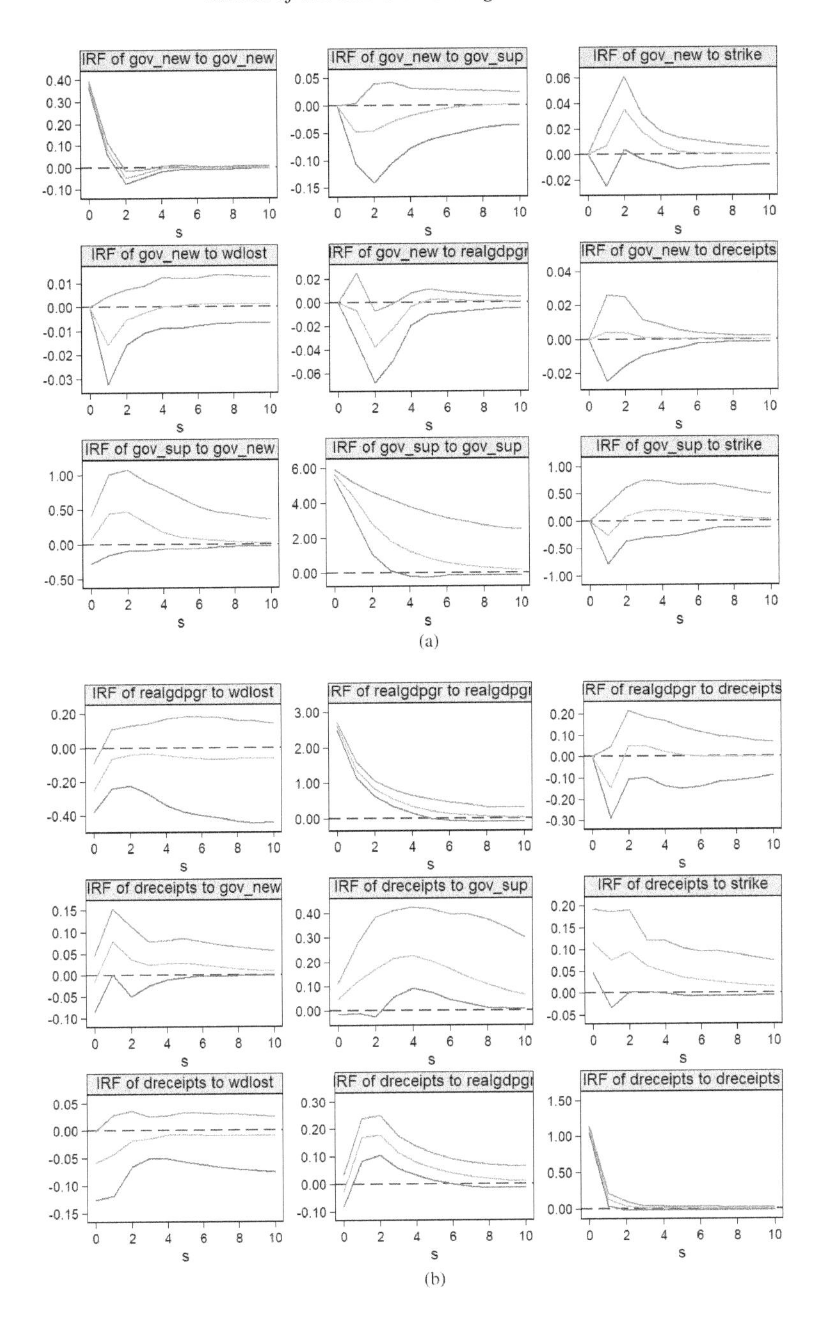

Figure 2. Impulse responses for 2 lag VAR of *gov_new, gov_sup, strike, wdlost, realgdpr, dreceipts* (generated by Monte-Carlo with 200 reps).

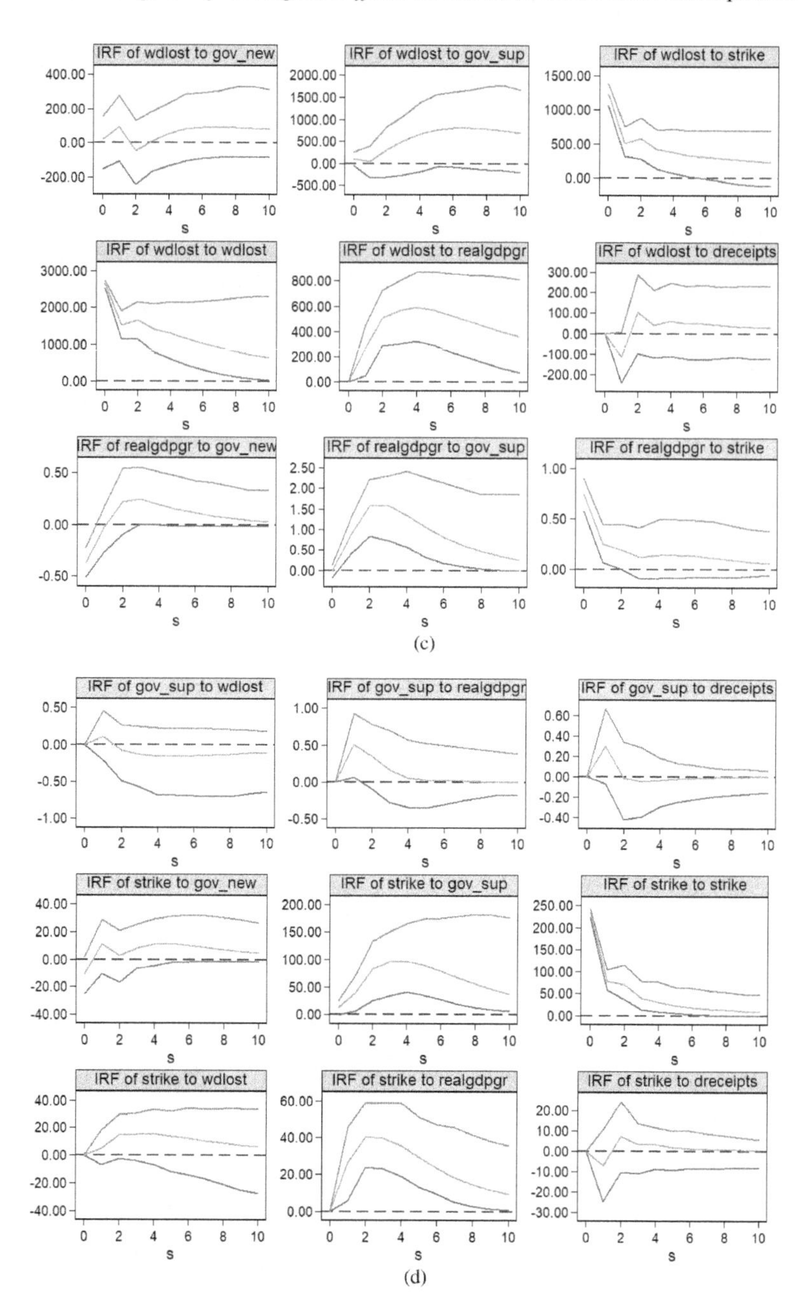

Figure 2. *(Continued)*

order: *gov_new, wdlost, strike, realgdpr, dreceipts.* The results are illustrated in Figures A.1 and A.2 in the Appendix, which reveal that ideological turnover has no significant impact on strike index, but *strike* has a lagged effect on ideological turnover.

6.3. *Robustness test 3*

In view of other important economic factors such as inflation rate and unemployment rate, we ran two further tests. However, we have to keep the number of variables in the system under six, due to the drastic decrease in the degrees of freedom and the constraints of the PVAR code. First, we display the impulse response functions of the model *gov_new, strike, wdlost, inflation, realgdpr, dreceipts* based on the relevant results (Anyon, 2005; Tarrow, 2011), considering that inflation is often referred to as a significant factor which can account for strikes and government change (Figure A.3 in the Appendix).

Second, we analyze the impulse response function of the ordering *gov_new, strike, wdlost, realgdpr, dreceipts, unemployment rate*, since *unemp* is also a classical variable affecting ideological turnover (Figure A.4 in the Appendix). These two tests show that there was no significant difference in the impulse response graph concerning our variables of interest, which would confirm the robustness of the previous results in this chapter.

7. Discussion and Conclusion

The results of the chapter indicated that the relationship between strikes and ideological turnover is much more complex than we thought. Through the innovative combination of the PVAR model with the panel data and the impulse response analysis, we found that strikes have a significant lagged effect on ideological turnover, which means that the effect in the immediate first period is not significant but the impact in the second and third years are significant. Besides, the effect is gradually weakened with further ideological turnover. On the other hand, the ideological turnover does not have a significant effect on strikes, neither current nor lagged.

At the level of methodology, the findings of this study enrich the methods used to further explore the casual mechanism in social science. Although this exploration has been the scholarly focus in previous studies, the complexity of social science calls for scholars to reassess their current conclusions about the casual mechanism, especially those conclusions that are "ahistorical" and ignore the temporality (Rast, 2012).

From the perspective of theory, the findings of this chapter are conducive to deepening the understanding of the mechanisms of strikes and ideological turnover. It is suggested here that both strikes and ideological turnover have self-reinforcing mechanisms, and that ideological turnover causes economic instability and future indirect social costs, which, to some extent, corresponds to the economic voting theory (Hansford & Gomez, 2015; Powell & Whitten, 1993). Our conclusions also provide a theoretical basis for the prediction of future government turnovers by evaluating the index of strike in different countries.

However, there are still some areas where we need to make further improvements. First, our conclusions are drawn on the basis of data from only 20 countries for the period from 1960 to 2014, so future research could test the applicability of these conclusions in more countries. The limitations of the dataset also lead to insufficient distinction between political systems and historical cultures in different countries, each of which has a potential impact on the results. Second, the number of strikes is taken as the alternative variable for social movements, but Rucht and Neidhardt (2002) have argued that the continuation of differentiation processes and the subsequent integration problems in modern societies increase the likelihood that social movements will emerge and become stabilized. The "Movement Society" is approaching. Therefore, modern social movements do not exclusively mean strikes but may include many new types of movements, such as student movements, environmental protection movements, anti-nuclear movements, and feminist movements, which impact greatly on politics. However, due to data limitation, the impact of these new types of social movements on politics has not yet been taken into account in this chapter (Anyon, 2005; Touraine, 1985).

Third, future research needs to explore further the directional impact of strikes on ideological turnover, i.e., whether strikes result in a left-wing to right-wing turnover or in right-wing to left-wing turnover. In addition, strikes are not self-contained, on the contrary, they work in coalition with other movements and influence other movements through their effects. More efforts need to be expended to observe whether movements that are occurring simultaneously in neighboring countries have movement-to-movement influences (Meyer & Whittier, 1994) and how the movement-to-movement influences impact on ideological turnover in different countries.

Last but not the least, measuring "working days lost from strikes" may not be the best way to judge the social costs of strikes, because it implicitly assumes that all the production and income which would normally generate are "lost" during a strike. However, companies may, at least partly, offset the losses in production and income during strikes by stockpiling inventories in anticipation of strikes, by production from workers in other companies that are not on strike, and by additional production following the end of strikes. As a result, there is likely to be a systematic upward bias in the measurement of the "net" social costs of strikes. Meanwhile, there are some potentially important variables that are omitted from the models in our research. For instance, government change is a result of many economic, political, and cultural forces other than those forces related to labor conflicts. Moreover, there has also been a phenomenon where a sharp decline in union membership, union power, and collective bargaining occurred in many of the countries. So, in short, our results do not mean that strikes have become more important than other factors in this period as a source of change in governments. Instead, we suggest that activity level of strikes affects ideological turnover with lags. Further investigation on the other factors causing political turnovers should be conducted.

Appendix A

Table A.1. The matrix of coefficients of variables.

	Strike	Working days lost	Ideological turnover	Real GDP growth	Unemployment rate	Receipts	Inflation	Government support
Strike	1							
Working days lost	0.4645	1						
Ideological turnover	0.0541	−0.0389	1					
Real GDP growth	0.112	0.0714	−0.1004	1				
Unemployment rate	−0.0459	0.0161	−0.0042	−0.2225	1			
Receipts	−0.2312	−0.3529	0.1368	−0.2677	0.1177	1		
Inflation	0.4306	0.1198	0.1437	0.0063	−0.1973	−0.1182	1	
Government support	0.0152	−0.0861	−0.0806	0.0271	−0.0805	−0.1814	0.0537	1

Note: The coefficient between working days lost and strikes is 0.4653. This suggests that they can be used concurrently in the model to analyze the impact of strikes or ideological turnover on the social costs.

Table A.2. The results of the unit root test.

	ADF test		IPS test	
	Test statistics	*P* value	Test statistics	*P* value
Strike	105.4866	0.0000	−11.2596	0.0000
Working days lost	87.7598	0.0000	−5.2176	0.0000
Government support	152.4502	0.0000	−7.1861	0.0000
Number of industrial disputes	95.9301	0.0000	—	—
Real GDP growth	154.8545	0.0000	−5.3737	0.0000
Receipts	111.6685	0.0000	−1.6734	0.2371
Dreceipts	162.2598	0.0000	−6.3019	0.0000
Unemp	128.4373	0.0000	−1.5217	0.4585
Dunemp	166.1531	0.0000	−4.5915	0.0000

Notes: The stability of the data needs to be tested before the construction of the PVAR model. The results of the unit root test indicate that receipts and unemp are I (1) series under the IPS test, while all the other variables are stable. Constraint data of the number of industrial disputes cannot meet the requirement of the IPS test.

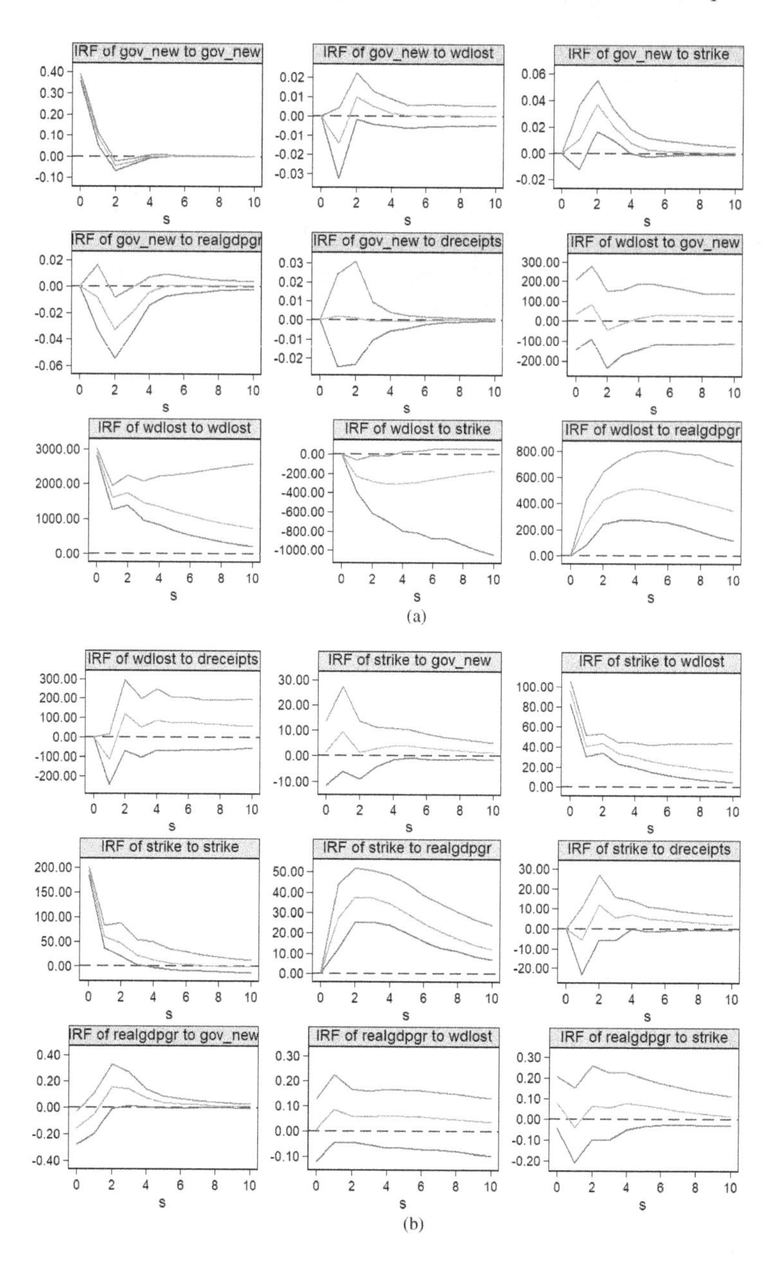

Figure A.1. Impulse responses for 2 lag VAR of *gov_new, wdlost, strike, realgdpr, dreceipts* (generated by Monte-Carlo with 200 reps).

Notes: The order of variables impacts on the results of impulse response, and Figure. A.1 displays the results of impulse response with the ordering of variables being *gov_new, wdlost, strike, realgdpr, dreceipts*. The results in Figure A.1 are in accordance with those in the earlier part of our study, demonstrating that the results of this chapter are explanatory.

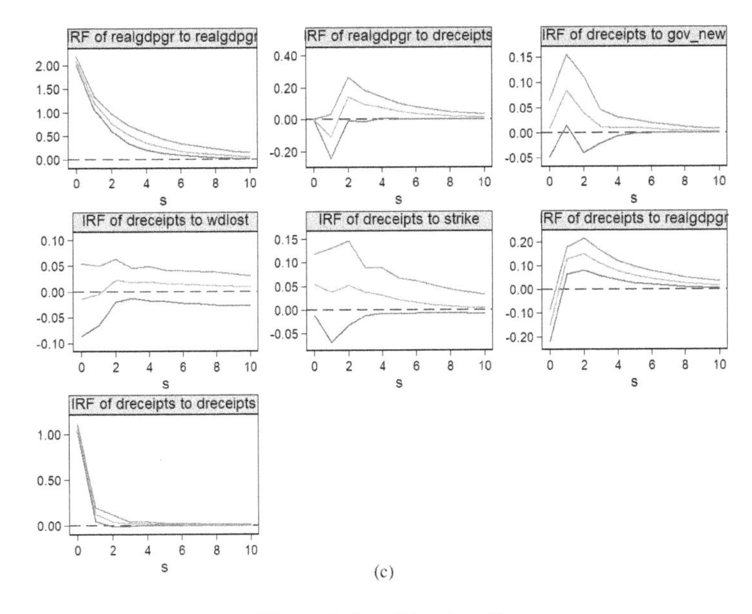

(c)

Figure A.1. (*Continued*)

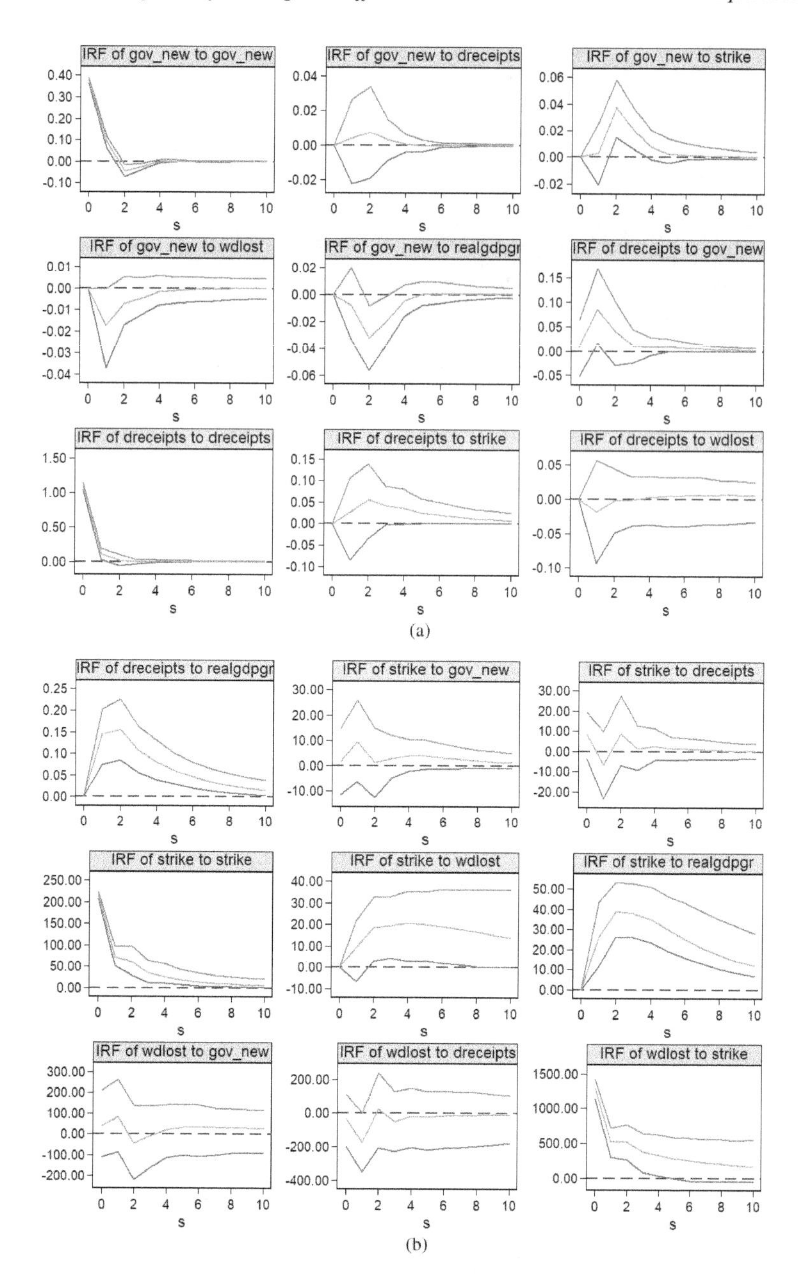

Figure A.2. Impulse responses for 2 lag VAR of *gov_new, dreceipts, strike, wdlost, realgdpr* (generated by Monte-Carlo with 200 reps).

Notes: Figure A.2 illustrates the results of impulse response with the ordering of variables order being *gov_new, dreceipts, strike, wdlost, realgdpr.* The results in Figure A.2 are highly consistent with those in our paper.

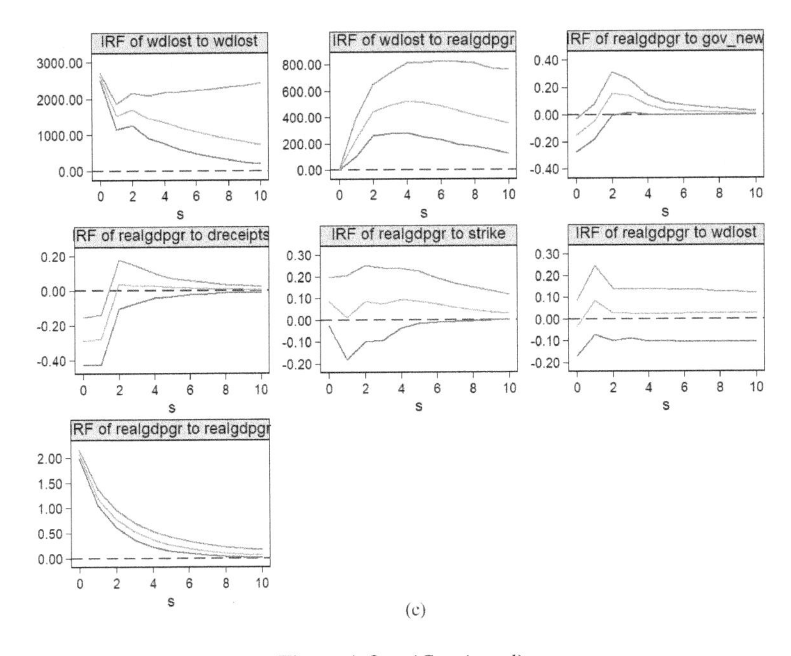

(c)

Figure A.2. (*Continued*)

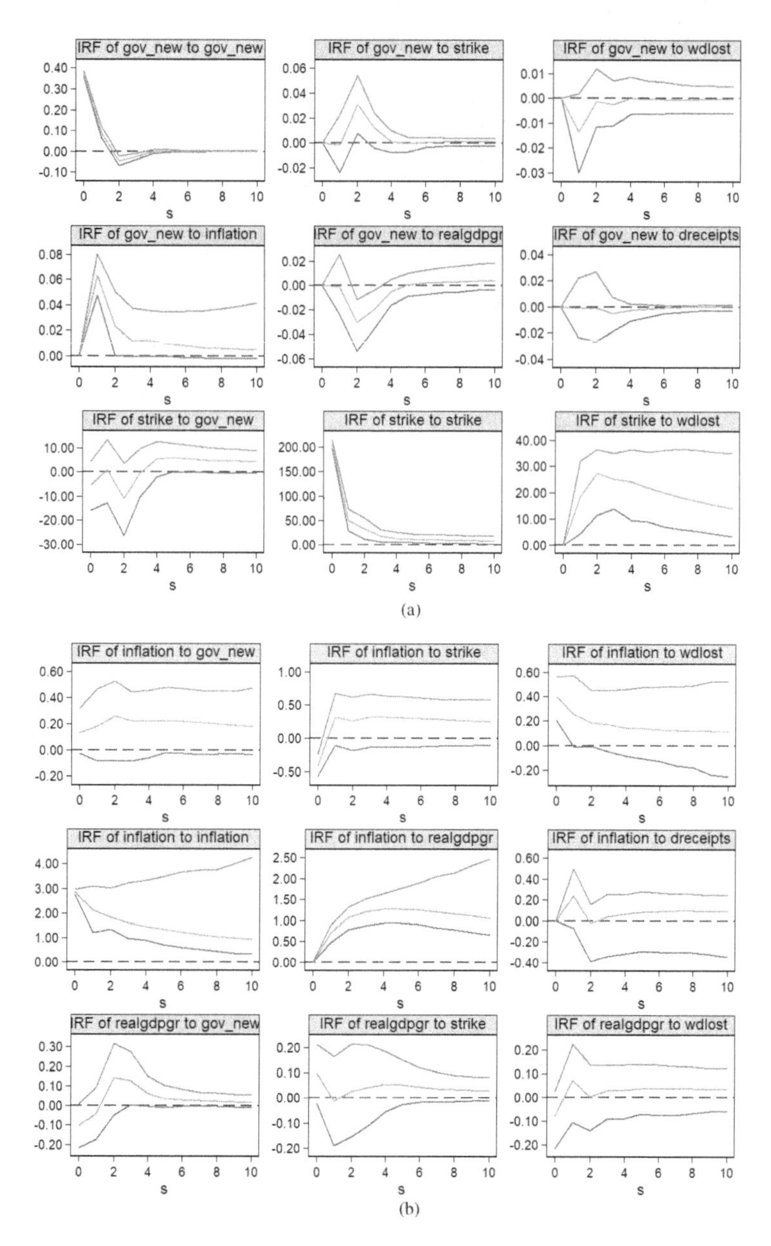

Figure A.3. Impulse responses for 2 lag VAR of *gov_new, strike, wdlost, inflation, realgdpr, dreceipts* (generated by Monte-Carlo with 200 reps).

Notes: Figure A.3 shows the results of impulse response with the ordering of variables being *gov_new, strike, wdlost, inflation, realgdpr, dreceipts*. The results in Figure A.3 are in line with those of our study.

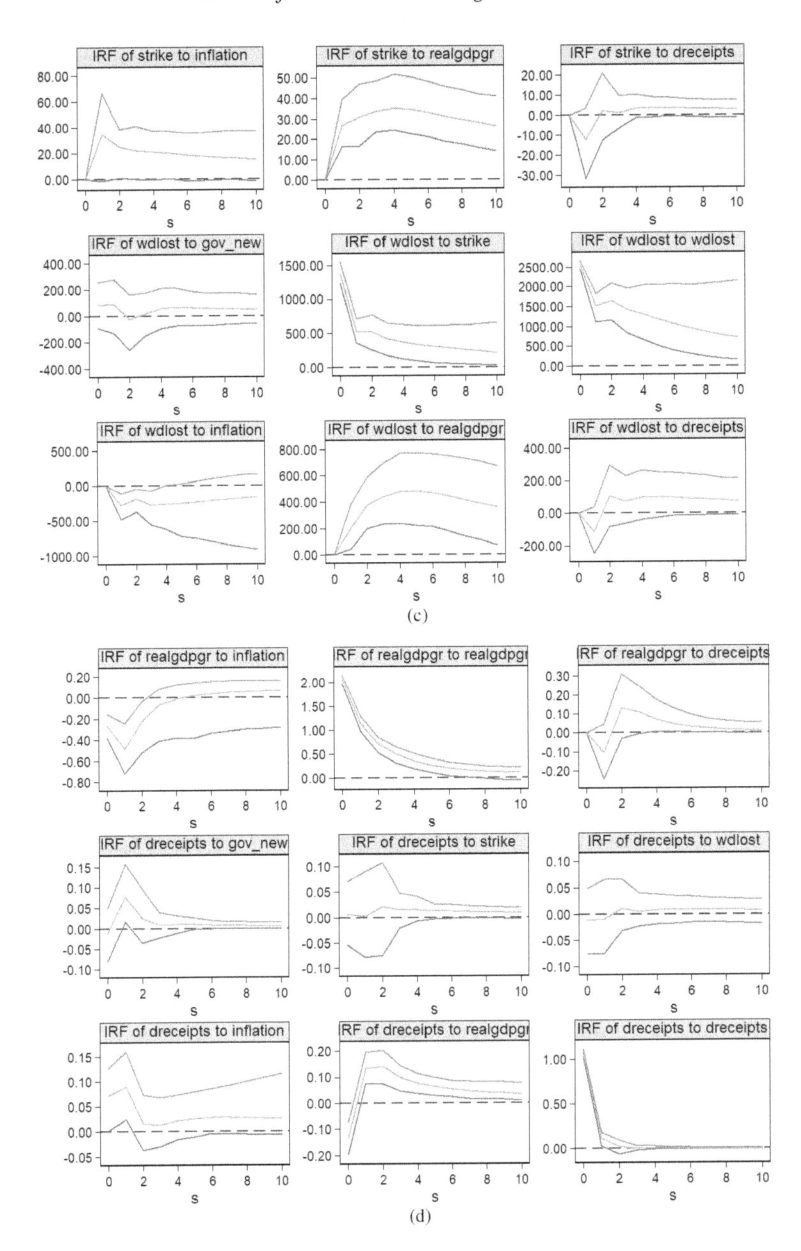

Figure A.3. *(Continued)*

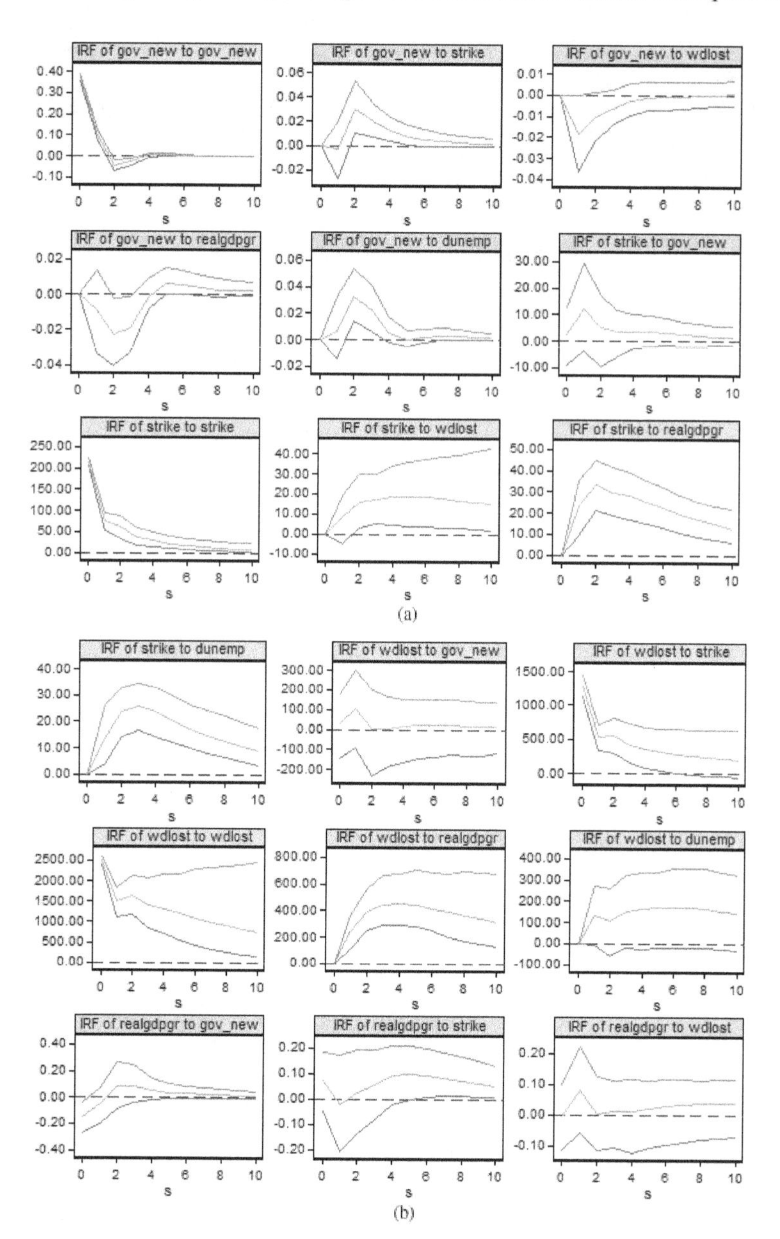

Figure A.4. Impulse responses for 2 lag VAR of *gov_new, strike, wdlost, realgdpr, dunemp* (generated by Monte-Carlo with 200 reps).

Notes: Figure A.4 describes the results of impulse response with the ordering of variables being *gov_new, strike, wdlost, realgdpr, dunemp.* The results in Figure A.4 are highly consistent with those in the chapter.

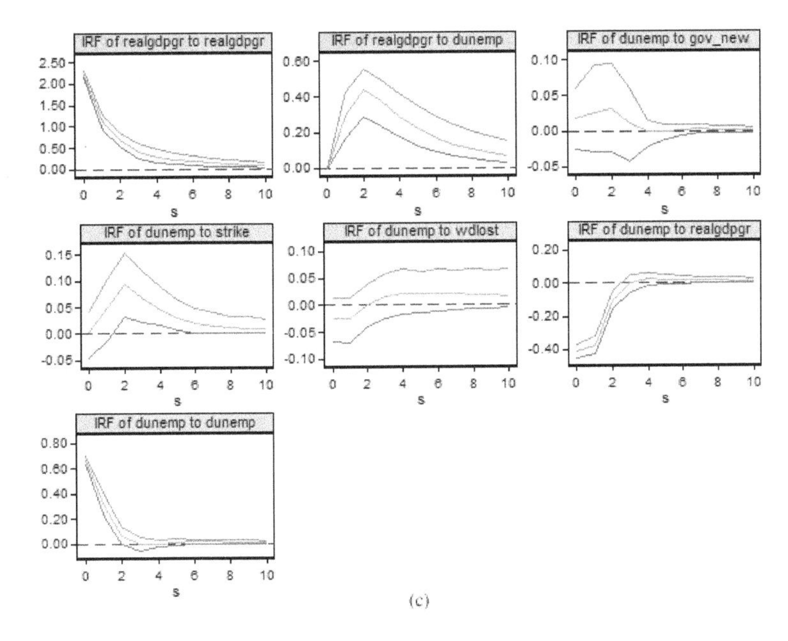

(c)

Figure A.4. (*Continued*)

Bibliography

Abrahamson, E. (1997). The emergence and prevalence of employee management rhetorics: The effects of long waves, labor unions, and turnover, 1875 to 1992. *Academy of Management Journal, 40*(3), 491–533.

Acemoglu, D., Johnson, S., & Robinson, J. A. (2002). Reversal of fortune: Geography and institutions in the making of the modern world income distribution. *The Quarterly Journal of Economics, 117*(4), 1231–1294.

Acemoglu, D., Johnson, S., & Robinson, J. A. (2005). Institutions as a fundamental cause of long-run growth. *Handbook of Economic Growth, 1*, 385–472.

Achen, C. H., & Bartels, L. M. (2016). *Democracy for Realists: Why Elections Do Not Produce Responsive Government*. Princeton: Princeton University Press.

Afonso, A. (2015). Choosing whom to betray: Populist right-wing parties, welfare state reforms and the trade-off between office and votes. *European Political Science Review, 7*(2), 271–292.

Afonso, A., & Papadopoulos, I. (2013). Right-wing populism, party polarisation and welfare state reforms in Switzerland (1994–2010). *SSRN Electronic Journal.*

Aizenman, J., & Marion, N. P. (1993). Policy uncertainty, persistence and growth. *Review of International Economics, 1*(2), 145–163.

Alesina, A., Özler, S., Roubini, N., & Swagel, P. (1996). Political instability and economic growth. *Journal of Economic Growth, 1*(2), 189–211.

Alesina, A., & Perotti, R. (1996). Income distribution, political instability, and investment. *European Economic Review, 40*(6), 1203–1228.

Alesina, A., Rosenthal, H., Calvert, R., & Eggertsson, T. (1995). *Partisan Politics Divided Government & Economy*. Cambridge: Cambridge University Press.

Alesina, A., Roubini, N., & Cohen, G. D. (1997). *Political Cycles and the Macroeconomy*. Cambridge: MIT press.

Allan, J. P., & Scruggs, L. (2004). Political partisanship and welfare state reform in advanced industrial societies. *American Journal of Political Science, 48*(3), 496–512.

Alt, J. E., & Lassen, D. D. (2006). Transparency, political polarization, and political budget cycles in OECD countries. *American Journal of Political Science, 50*(3), 530–550.

Amable, B., Gatti, D., & Schumacher, J. (2006). Welfare state retrenchment: The partisan effect revisited. *Oxford Review of Economic Policy, 22*(3), 426–444.

Amenta, E., & Zylan, Y. (1991). It happened here: Political opportunity, the new institutionalism, and the Townsend movement. *American Sociological Review*, 250–265.

Anyon, J. (2005). *Radical Possibilities: Public Policy, Urban Education, and a New Social Movement*. London: Routledge.

Armingeon, K., Isler, C., Knöpfel, L., Weisstanner, D., & Engler, S. (2016). Codebook: Comparative political data set 1960–2014. *Working Paper*. Institute of Political Science, University of Berne.

Armingeon, K., & Schädel, L. (2015). Social inequality in political participation: The dark sides of individualisation. *West European Politics, 38*(1), 1–27.

Arzheimer, K., & Carter, E. (2006). Political opportunity structures and right-wing extremist party success. *European Journal of Political Research, 45*(3), 419–443.

Bai, J., & Perron, P. (1998). Estimating and testing linear models with multiple structural changes. *Econometrica, 66*(1), 47–78.

Bai, J., & Perron, P. (2003). Computation and analysis of multiple structural change models. *Journal of Applied Econometrics, 18*(1), 1–22.

Bailar, B. A. (1989). Information needs, surveys, and measurement errors. In Kasprzyk, D., Duncan, G. J., Kalton, G., & Singh, M. P. (Eds.), *Panel Surveys*. New York: John Wiley & Sons.

Baker, S. R., Bloom, N., Canes-Wrone, B., Davis, S. J., & Rodden, J. (2014). Why has US policy uncertainty risen since 1960? *The American Economic Review, 104*(5), 56–60.

Banks, A. S., & Wilson, K. A. (2013). *Cross-National Time-Series Data Archive*. edited by Databanks International. Jerusalem, Israel.

Banks, A. S., & Wilson, K. A. (2017). *Cross-National Time-Series Data Archive*. Databanks International. Jerusalem, Israel; see https://www.cntsdata.com/.

Bates, R. H., & Block, S. (2011). Political institutions and agricultural trade interventions in Africa. *American Journal of Agricultural Economics, 93*(2), 317–323.

Bay, A.-H., Finseraas, H., & Pedersen, A. W. (2013). Welfare dualism in two scandinavian welfare states: Public opinion and party politics. *West European Politics, 36*(1), 199–220.

Bell, D. (1962). *The End of Ideology: On the Exhaustion of Political Ideas in the Fifties, with "The Resumption of History in the New Century"*. Cambridge: Harvard University Press.

Bertelli, A. (2006). The role of political ideology in the structural design of new governance agencies. *Public Administration Review, 66*(4), 583–595.

Binder, S. A. (1996). The partisan basis of procedural choice: Allocating parliamentary rights in the house, 1789–1990. *American Political Science Review, 90*(1), 8–20.

Bingham Powell Jr, G. (2009). The ideological congruence controversy: The impact of alternative measures, data, and time periods on the effects of election rules. *Comparative Political Studies, 42*(12), 1475–1497.

Birchfield, V., & Crepaz, M. M. L. (1998). The impact of constitutional structures and collective and competitive veto points on income inequality in industrialized democracies. *European Journal of Political Research, 34*(2), 175–200.

Bjørnskov, C. (2008). The growth–inequality association: Government ideology matters. *Journal of Development Economics, 87*(2), 300–308.

Bloom, N. (2014). Fluctuations in uncertainty. *The Journal of Economic Perspectives, 28*(2), 153–175.

Blumer, H. (1995). *Social Movements*. UK: Palgrave Macmillan.

Bobick, T., & Smith, A. (2013). The impact of leader turnover on the onset and the resolution of WTO disputes. *Review of International Organizations, 8*(4), 423–445.

Bohlmann, H. R., Van Heerden, J. H., Dixon, P., & Rimmer, M. (2015). The impact of the 2014 platinum mining strike in South Africa: An economy-wide analysis. *Economic Modelling, 51*, 403–411.

Boräng, F., Nistotskaya, M., & Xezonakis, G. (2017). The quality of government determinants of support for democracy. *Journal of Public Affairs, 17*(1–2), 1643.

Box, G. E. (1953). Non-normality and tests on variances. *Biometrika, 40*(3/4), 318–335.

Bradley, D., & Stephens, J. D. (2001). Distribution and redistribution in postindustrial democracies. *World Politics, 55*(2), 193–228.

Bradley, D. H., & Stephens, J. D. (2007). Employment performance in OECD countries: A test of Neoliberal and Institutionalist hypotheses. *Comparative Political Studies, 40*(12), 1486–1510.

Brana, S., Djigbenou, M. L., & Prat, S. (2012). Global excess liquidity and asset prices in emerging countries: A PVAR approach. *Emerging Markets Review, 13*(3), 256–267.

Brender, A., & Drazen, A. (2005). Political budget cycles in new versus established democracies. *Journal of Monetary Economics, 52*(7), 1271–1295.

Brunk, G. G., & Minehart, T. G. (1984). How important is elite turnover to policy change? *American Journal of Political Science, 28*(3), 559–569.

Budge, I. (2001). *Mapping Policy Preferences: Estimates for Parties, Electors, and Governments, 1945–1998* (Vol. 1). Oxford: Oxford University Press on Demand.

Budge, I., Ezrow, L., & Mcdonald, M. D. (2010). Ideology, party factionalism and policy change: An integrated dynamic theory. *British Journal of Political Science, 40*(4), 781–804.

Budge, I., & Hofferbert, R. I. (1990). Mandates and policy outputs: U.S. party platforms and federal expenditures. *American Political Science Review, 84*(1), 111–131.

Budge, I., & Laver, M. J. (2016). *Party Policy and Government Coalitions*. London: Springer.

Bunce, V. (1980). Changing leaders and changing policies: The impact of elite succession on budgetary priorities in democratic countries. *American Journal of Political Science, 24*(3), 373–395.

Bunce, V. (2014). *Do New Leaders Make a Difference? Executive Succession and Public Policy Under Capitalism and Socialism*. Princeton: Princeton University Press.

Burke, W. W., & Litwin, G. H. (1992). A causal model of organizational performance and change. *Journal of Management, 18*(3), 523–545.

Busemeyer, M. R., & Garritzmann, J. L. (2017). Public opinion on policy and budgetary trade-offs in European welfare states: Evidence from a new comparative survey. *Journal of European Public Policy, 24*(4), 1–19.

Butler, D. M., Volden, C., Dynes, A. M., & Shor, B. (2017). Ideology, learning, and policy diffusion: Experimental evidence. *American Journal of Political Science, 61*(1), 37–49.

Campolieti, M., Hebdon, R., & Dachis, B. (2014). The impact of collective bargaining legislation on strike activity and wage settlements. *Industrial Relations: A Journal of Economy and Society, 53*(3), 394–429.

Canes-Wrone, B., Clark, T. S., & Park, J.-K. (2012). Judicial independence and retention elections. *Journal of Law, Economics, and Organization, 28*(2), 211–234.

Canes-Wrone, B., & Park, J.-K. (2012). Electoral business cycles in OECD countries. *American Political Science Review, 106*(01), 103–122.

Carbone, G., & Pellegata, A. (2016). Researching the dynamics of leaders' replacement: The Africa Leadership Change (ALC) dataset. *European Political Science, 17*(2), 1–24.

Carmines, E. G., & D'Amico, N. J. (2014). The new look in political ideology research. *Annual Review of Political Science, 18*(1), 205–216.

Cheibub, J. A. (2002). Minority presidents, deadlock situations, and the survival of presidential democracies. *Comparative Political Studies, 35*(3), 284–312.

Cheibub, J. A., & Przeworski, A. (2004). Government coalitions and legislative success under presidentialism and parliamentarism. *British Journal of Political Science, 34*(4), 565–587.

Cheibub, J. A., Przeworski, A., & Saiegh, S. (2002). Government Coalitions under Presidentialism and Parliamentarism. *Dados, 45*(2), 187–218.

Chow, G. C. (1960). Tests of equality between sets of coefficients in two linear regressions. *Econometrica: Journal of the Econometric Society, 28*(3), 591–605.

Clemente, J., Montanes, A., & Reyes, M. (1998). Testing for a unit root in variables with a double change in the mean. *Economics Letters, 59*(2), 175–182.

Clinton, J. D., & Lapinski, J. S. (2006). Measuring legislative accomplishment, 1877–1994. *American Journal of Political Science, 50*(1), 232–249.

Coleman, J. J. (1999). Unified government, divided government, and party responsiveness. *American Political Science Review, 93*(4), 821–835.

Coppedge, M., Gerring, J., Lindberg, S. I., Skaaning, S. E., Teorell, J., & Altman, D., *et al.* (2016). V-dem dataset v6.2. SSRN Electronic Journal.

Cutler, L. N. (1988). Some reflections about divided government. *Presidential Studies Quarterly, 18*(3), 485–492.

Dahlberg, S., Holmberg, S., Rothstein, B., Hartmann, F., & Svensson, R. (2016). The Quality of Government Basic Dataset, version Jan16. *University of Gothenburg: The Quality of Government Institute. Retrieved form* http:// www/. *qog. pol. gu. se doi, 10.*

De Mesquita, B. B., & Smith, A. (2010). Leader survival, revolutions, and the nature of government finance. *American Journal of Political Science, 54*(4), 936–950.

Devereux, P. J., & Hart, R. A. (2011). A good time to stay out? Strikes and the business cycle. *British Journal of Industrial Relations, 49*(s1), 70–92.

Dewan, T., & Hortala-Vallve, R. (2011). The three as of government formation: Appointment, allocation, and assignment. *American Journal of Political Science, 55*(3), 610–627.

Diamond, J. (1997). *Germs, Guns, and Steel: The Fates of Human Societies.* NY: Norton.

Dickey, D. A., & Fuller, W. A. (1979). Distribution of the estimators for autoregressive time series with a unit root. *Journal of the American Statistical Association, 74*(366a), 427–431.

Diermeier, D., Eraslan, H., & Merlo, A. (2002). Coalition governments and comparative constitutional design *European Economic Review, 46*(4–5), 893–907.

Dixon, John, E. (1992). *Social Welfare in Socialist Countries.* London: Routledge.

Dodd, L. (2015). *Coalitions in Parliamentary Government.* London: Princeton University Press.

Douglass, C. North (1981). *Structure and Change in Economic History.* New York: Norton.

Downs, A. (1957). An economic theory of political action in a democracy. *Journal of Political Economy, 65*(2), 135–150.

Drazen, A. (2001). The political business cycle after 25 years *NBER Macroeconomics Annual 2000*, Vol. 15. Cambridge: MIT Press, pp. 75–138.

Dreher, A., & Jensen, N. M. (2009). Country or leader? Political change and UN General Assembly voting. *European Journal of Political Economy, 29*(3), 183–196.

Driscoll, J. C., & Kraay, A. C. (1998). Consistent covariance matrix estimation with spatially dependent panel data. *Review of Economics & Statistics, 80*(4), 549–560.

Earle, J. S., & Gehlbach, S. (2015). The productivity consequences of political turnover: Firm-level evidence from Ukraine's orange revolution. *American Journal of Political Science, 59*(3), 708–723.

Easterly, W., & Levine, R. (1997). Africa's growth tragedy: Policies and ethnic divisions. *The Quarterly Journal of Economics, 112*(4), 1203–1250.

Efthyvoulou, G. (2012). Political budget cycles in the European Union and the impact of political pressures. *Public Choice, 153*(3–4), 295–327.

Elbahnasawy, N. G., Ellis, M. A., & Adom, A. D. (2016). Political instability and the informal economy. *World Development, 85*, 31–42.

Elgie, R. (2001). *Divided Government in Comparative Perspective.* Oxford: Oxford University Press.

Elgin, C. (2010). Political turnover, taxes and the shadow economy. *Bogazici University Department of Economics Working Papers, 8.*

Esping-Andersen, G. (1990). *The Three Worlds of Welfare Capitalism.* Cambridge: Polity Press.

Estévez-Abe, M. (2008). *Welfare and Capitalism in Postwar Japan.* Cambridge: Cambridge University Press.

Fatás, A., & Mihov, I. (2013). Policy volatility, institutions, and economic growth. *Review of Economics and Statistics, 95*(2), 362–376.

Feldman, S., & Zaller, J. (1992). The political culture of ambivalence: Ideological responses to the welfare state. *American Journal of Political Science, 36*(1), 268.

Feng, Y. (2001). Political freedom, political instability, and policy uncertainty: A study of political institutions and private investment in developing countries. *International Studies Quarterly, 45*(2), 271–294.

Ferguson, T., & Voth, H.-J. (2008). Betting on Hitler — the value of political connections in Nazi Germany. *The Quarterly Journal of Economics, 123*(1), 101–137.

Fingleton, B. (1999). Spurious spatial regression: Some Monte Carlo results with a spatial unit root and spatial cointegration. *Journal of Regional Science, 39*(1), 1–19.

Finkelstein, S., & Hambrick, D. C. (1990). Top-management-team tenure and organizational outcomes: The moderating role of managerial discretion. *Administrative Science Quarterly, 35*(3), 484–503.

Fiorina, M. P. (1991). Divided government in the States. *PS: Political Science & Politics, 24*(4), 646.

Flacks, R. (1970). The revolt of the advantaged: An exploration of the roots of student protest. *Learning About Politics: A Reader in Political Socialization.* New York: Random House, pp. 182–191.

Fosu, A. K. (2002). Political instability and economic growth. *American Journal of Economics and Sociology, 61*(1), 329–348.

Franzese Jr, R. J. (2002). Electoral and partisan cycles in economic policies and outcomes. *Annual Review of Political Science, 5*(1), 369–421.

Franzosi, R. (1989). One hundred years of strike statistics: Methodological and theoretical issues in quantitative strike research. *ILR Review, 42*(3), 348–362.

Fukuyama, F. (2006). *The End of History and the Last Man.* New York: Simon and Schuster.

Gandhi, J., & Przeworski, A. (2007). Authoritarian institutions and the survival of autocrats. *Comparative Political Studies, 40*(11), 1279–1301.

Garmann, S. (2014). Do government ideology and fragmentation matter for reducing CO_2-emissions? Empirical evidence from OECD countries. *Ecological Economics, 105*(9), 1–10.

Gasparyan, O. T. (2015). Institutional factors of government efficiency: Cross-country comparative analysis. *Social Science Electronic Publishing, 37*(5), 587–600.

Geller, D. S. (1982). Economic modernization and political instability in Latin America: A causal analysis of bureaucratic-authoritarianism. *Political Research Quarterly, 35*(1), 33–49.

George, V., & Wilding, P. (1985). *Ideology and Social Welfare*. New York: Psychology Press.

Gersovitz, M., & Paxson, C. H. (1996). The revenues and expenditures of African governments: Modalities and consequences. *Journal of African Economies, 5*(2), 199–227.

Giddens, A. (1999). *The Third Way: The Renewal of Social Democracy*. Cambridge: Polity Press.

Goemans, H., Gleditsch, K. S., & Chiozza, G. (2009). Archigos: A data set on leaders, 1875–2004, version 2.9. University of Rochester.

Goldstone, J. (2003). *States, Parties, and Social Movements*. Cambridge: Cambridge University Press.

Gould, A. C. (2001). Party size and policy outcomes: An empirical analysis of taxation in democracies. *Studies in Comparative International Development, 36*(2), 3–26.

Graen, G., Novak, M. A., & Sommerkamp, P. (1982). The effects of leader — member exchange and job design on productivity and satisfaction: Testing a dual attachment model. *Organizational Behavior and Human Performance, 30*(1), 109–131.

Gray, J., & Kucik, J. (2017). Leadership turnover and the durability of international trade commitments. *Comparative Political Studies*, 001041401769533.

Greene, Z., & Jensen, C. B. (2016). Manifestos, salience and junior ministerial appointments. *Party Politics, 22*(3), 382–392.

Griliches, Z., & Hausman, J. A. (1984). Errors in variables in panel data. *Journal of Econometrics, 31*(1), 93–118.

Ha, E. (2015). The impact of democracy, government ideology, and globalization on social spending in less developed countries. *International Journal of Comparative Sociology, 56*(5), 338–365.

Habermas, J. (1971). *Toward a Rational Society: Student Protest, Science, and Politics*, Vol. 404. Boston: Beacon Press.

Hamilton, J. D. (1994). *Time Series Analysis*, Vol. 2. Princeton: Princeton University Press, pp. 690–696.

Han, K. J. (2015). When will left-wing governments introduce liberal migration policies? An implication of power resources theory. *International Studies Quarterly, 59*(3), pp. 602–614.

Hansford, T. G., & Gomez, B. T. (2015). Reevaluating the sociotropic economic voting hypothesis. *Electoral Studies, 39*, 15–25.

Häusermann, S., Picot, G., & Geering, D. (2013). Review article: Rethinking party politics and the welfare state — recent advances in the literature. *British Journal of Political Science, 43*(1), 221–240.

Heckman, J. (1990). Varieties of selection bias. *The American Economic Review, 80*(2), 313–318.

Hibbs, D. A. (1977). Political parties and macroeconomic policy. *American Political Science Review, 71*(04), 1467–1487.

Hibbs, D. A. (1987). *The Political Economy of Industrial Democracies*. Cambridge: Harvard University Press.

Hicks, A. M., & Swank, D. H. (1992). Politics, institutions and welfare spending in industrialized democracies, 1960–1982. *American Political Science Review, 86*(3), 658–674.

Hicks, T. (2011). *Strategic Partisanship and Left-wing Policy Efficiency*. Social Science Electronic Publishing, New York.

Hindess, B. (1996). No end of ideology. *History of the Human Sciences, 9*(2), 79–98.

Hoechle, D. (2007). Robust standard errors for panel regressions with cross–sectional dependence. *Stata Journal, 7*(3), 281–312.

Holtz-Eakin, D., Newey, W., & Rosen, H. S. (1988). Estimating vector autoregressions with panel data. *Econometrica, 56*(6), 1371–1395.

Hooghe, L., Marks, G., & Wilson, C. J. (2002). Does left/right structure party positions on European integration? *Comparative Political Studies, 35*(8), 965–989.

Horowitz, S., Hoff, K., & Milanovic, B. (2009). Government turnover: Concepts, measures and applications. *European Journal of Political Research, 48*(1), 107–129.

Howell, W., Adler, S., Cameron, C., & Riemann, C. (2000). Divided government and the legislative productivity of Congress, 1945–94. *Legislative Studies Quarterly, 25*(2), 285.

Huber, E., & Stephens, J. D. (2001). *Development and Crisis of the Welfare State: Parties and Policies in Global Markets*. Chicago: University of Chicago press.

Im, K. S., Pesaran, M. H., & Shin, Y. (2003). Testing for unit roots in heterogeneous panels. *Journal of Econometrics, 115*(1), 53–74.

Indridason, I. H., & Kam, C. (2008). Cabinet reshuffles and ministerial drift. *British Journal of Political Science, 38*(4), 621–656.

Inglehart, R., & Klingemann, H.-D. (1976). Party identification, ideological preference and the left-right dimension among Western mass publics. In: Budge, I., Crewe, I., & Farlie, D. (Eds.), *Party Identification and Beyond: Representations of Voting and Party Competition*. London: Wiley, 243–273.

Jeffrey, O., & Robbins, J. (1998). Social memory studies: From "Collective Memory" to the historical sociology of mnemonic practices. *Annual Review of Sociology, 24*(1), 105–140.

Jenkins, J. C., Jacobs, D., & Agnone, J. (2003). Political opportunities and African–American protest, 1948–1997. *American Journal of Sociology, 109*(2), 277–303.

Jensen, C. (2010). Issue compensation and right-wing government social spending. *European Journal of Political Research, 49*(2), 282–299.

Johnson, K. S. (1986). The portrayal of lame-duck presidents by the national print media. *Presidential Studies Quarterly*, *34*(4), 50–65.

Jones, B. F., & Olken, B. A. (2005). Do leaders matter? National leadership and growth since World War II. *The Quarterly Journal of Economics, 120*(3), 835–864.

Jones, D. R. (2001). Party polarization and legislative gridlock. *Political Research Quarterly, 54*(1), 125–141.

Jost, J. T. (2006). The end of the end of ideology. *American Psychologist, 61*(7), 651.

Kagan, R. (2009). *The Return of History and the End of Dreams*. New York: Vintage.

Kalton, G., Kasprzyk, D., & McMillen, D. (1989). Information needs, surveys, and measurement errors. *Panel Survey*. New York: Wiley, pp. 249–270.

Kane, T. M. (2007). Hot planet, cold wars: Climate change and ideological conflict. *Energy & Environment, 18*(5), 533–547.

Keefer, P. (2004). What does political economy tell us about economic development — and vice versa? *Annual Review of Political Science, 7*, 247–272.

Key, V. O. (1966). *The Responsible Electorate*. Cambridge: Belknap Press of Harvard University Press.

Kitao, S. (2014). A life-cycle model of unemployment and disability insurance. *Journal of Monetary Economics, 68*(1), 1–18.

Kitschelt, H., & Wilkinson, S. I. (2007). *Patrons, Clients and Policies: Patterns of Democratic Accountability and Political Competition*. Cambridge: Cambridge University Press.

Klingemann, H.-D. (2006). *Mapping Policy Preferences II: Estimates for Parties, Electors, and Governments in Eastern Europe, European Union, and OECD 1990–2003*, Vol. 2. Oxford: Oxford University Press on Demand.

Klomp, J., & Haan, J. D. (2013). Political budget cycles and election outcomes. *Public Choice, 157*(1–2), 245–267.

Knutsen, C. H., & Wig, T. (2015). Government turnover and the effects of regime type. *Comparative Political Studies, 48*(7), 882–914.

Koenker, D. P. (1981). *Moscow Workers and the 1917 Revolution.* Princeton: Princeton University Press.

König, T., & Luig, B. (2012). Party ideology and legislative agendas: Estimating contextual policy positions for the study of EU decision-making. *European Union Politics, 13*(4), 604–625.

Krause, S., & Méndez, F. (2003). Policy makers' preferences, party ideology, and the political business cycle. *Southern Economic Journal, 71*(4), 752–767.

Kriner, D., & Schwartz, L. (2008). Divided government and congressional investigations. *Legislative Studies Quarterly, 33*(2), 295–321.

Krutz, G. S. (2000). Getting around gridlock: The effect of omnibus utilization on legislative productivity. *Legislative Studies Quarterly, 25*(4), 533–549.

La Porta, R., Lopezdesilanes, F., Shleifer, A., & Vishny, R. (1999). The quality of government. *Journal of Law Economics & Organization, 15*(1), 222–279.

Lambert, J. B. (2005). *"If the Workers Took a Notion": The Right to Strike and American Political Development.* New York: Cornell University Press.

Lange, S. L. D., Festenstein, M., & Smith, M. (2012). *New Alliances: Why Mainstream Parties Govern with Radical Right-wing Populist Parties.*

Laver, M., & Shepsle, K. A. (1990a). Coalitions and cabinet government. *American Political Science Review, 84*(3), 873–890.

Laver, M., & Shepsle, K. A. (1990b). Government coalitions and intraparty politics. *British Journal of Political Science, 20*(4), 489–507.

Layton-Henry, Z. (2006). Doing research in political science. An introduction to comparative methods and statistics (Second Edition). *British Politics, 1*(2), 288–289.

Leonard, J. (1991). Divided government and dysfunctional politics. *PS: Political Science & Politics, 24*(4), 651–653.

Li, H., & Zhou, L.-A. (2005). Political turnover and economic performance: The incentive role of personnel control in China. *Journal of Public Economics, 89*(9), 1743–1762.

Lijphart, A. (2002). Patterns of democracy: Government forms and performance in 36 countries. *Politische Vierteljahresschrift, 42*(2), 335–337.

Linz, J. J., & Valenzuela, A. (1994). *The Failure of Presidential Democracy.* Baltimore: Johns Hopkins University Press.

Lister, R. (1991). Social security in the 1980s. *Social Policy & Administration, 25*(2), 91–107.

Lof, M., & Malinen, T. (2014). Does sovereign debt weaken economic growth? A panel VAR analysis. *Economics Letters, 122*(3), 403–407.

Londregan, J. B., & Poole, K. T. (1990). Poverty, the coup trap, and the seizure of executive power. *World Politics, 42*(2), 151–183.

Love, I., & Zicchino, L. (2006). Financial development and dynamic investment behavior: Evidence from panel VAR. *Quarterly Review of Economics & Finance, 46*(2), 190–210.

Lucifora, C., & Moriconi, S. (2015). Political instability and labour market institutions. *European Journal of Political Economy, 39*, 201–221.

Lusinyan, L., & Thornton, J. (2012). The intertemporal relation between government revenue and expenditure in the United Kingdom, 1750 to 2004. *Applied Economics, 44*(18), 2321–2333.

Luxemburg, R. (1925). *The Mass Strike, the Political Party, and the Trade Union*. Detroit: Marxian Education Society.

Mattes, M., Leeds, B. A., & Matsumura, N. (2016). Measuring change in source of leader support. *Journal of Peace Research, 53*(2), 259–267.

Mattoni, A. (2016). *Media Practices and Protest Politics: How Precarious Workers Mobilise*. New York: Routledge.

Mayhew, D. R. (1991). Divided party control: Does it make a difference? *PS: Political Science & Politics, 24*(4), 637.

Mayhew, D. R. (2005). *Divided We Govern: Party Control, Lawmaking, and Investigations, 1946–2002, Second Edition*. New Haven: Yale University Press.

McAdam, D., McCarthy, J. D., & Zald, M. N. (1996). *Comparative Perspectives on Social Movements: Political Opportunities, Mobilizing Structures, and Cultural Framings*. Cambridge: Cambridge University Press.

Mccubbins, M. D. (1991). Party governance and U.S. Budget deficits: Divided government and fiscal stalemate. *NBER Chapters*, 83–122.

Mcgillivray, F., & Smith, A. (2004). The impact of leadership turnover on trading relations between states. *International Organization, 58*(3), 567–600.

Menefee-Libey, D. (1991). Divided government as scapegoat. *PS: Political Science & Politics, 24*(4), 643.

Mesquita, B. B. D., & Smith, A. (2010). Leader survival, revolutions, and the nature of government finance. *American Journal of Political Science, 54*(4), 936–950.

Meyer, D. S., & Whittier, N. (1994). Social movement spillover. *Social Problems, 41*(2), 277–298.

Michaela Mattes, Ashleyleeds, B., & Royce Carroll. (2015). Leadership turnover and foreign policy change: Societal interests, domestic institutions, and voting in the United Nations. *Social Science Electronic Publishing, 59*(2), 280–290.

Midtbø, T. (1999). The impact of parties, economic growth, and public sector expansion: A comparison of long-term dynamics in the Scandinavian and Anglo–American democracies. *European Journal of Political Research, 35*(2), 199–223.

Milanovic, B., Hoff, K., & Horowitz, S. (2010). Turnover in power as a restraint on investing in influence: Evidence from the postcommunist transition. *Economics & Politics, 22*(3), 329–361.

Mizrahi, T., & Davis, L. (2008). *The Encyclopedia of Social Work: 4 Volume Set.* USA: OUP.

Moses, J. A. (2013). The great war as ideological conflict — An Australian perspective. *War & Society*, 7(2), 56–76.

Müller, W. C., & Kaare, S. (1999.). *Policy, Office, or Votes? How Political Parties in Western Europe Make Hard Decisions.* Cambridge: Cambridge University Press.

Narayan, P. K., & Narayan, S. (2006). Government revenue and government expenditure nexus: Evidence from developing countries. *Applied Economics, 38*(3), 285–291.

Neumayer, E. (2003). Are left-wing party strength and corporatism good for the environment? Evidence from panel analysis of air pollution in OECD countries. *Ecological Economics, 45*(2), 203–220.

Ng, I. (1991). Predictors of strike voting behavior: The case of university faculty. *Journal of Labor Research, 12*(2), 123–134.

Nordhaus, W. D. (1975). The political business cycle. *The Review of Economic Studies, 42*(2), 169–190.

North, D. C. (1990). *Institutions, Institutional Change, and Economic Performance.* Cambridge: Cambridge University Press.

North, D. C., & Weingast, B. R. (1989). Constitutions and commitment: The evolution of institutions governing public choice in seventeenth-century England. *The Journal of Economic History, 49*(4), 803–832.

Obinger, H., Schmitt, C., & Zohlnhoefer, R. (2014). Partisan politics and privatization in OECD countries. *Comparative Political Studies, 47*(9), 1294–1323.

Pearson, K. (2006). Note on regression and inheritance in the case of two parents. *Proceedings of the Royal Society of London, 58*, 240–242.

Perry, E. J. (2007). Studying Chinese politics: Farewell to revolution? *The China Journal*, 57, 1–22.

Persson, T., & Tabellini, G. E. (2002). Political economics: Explaining public policy. *Southern Economic Journal, 1*(1–2), 204–206.

Pierson, P. (2011). *Politics In Time: History, Institutions, and Social Analysis*. Princeton: Princeton University Press.

Pietersen, C., & Oni, O. (2014). Employee turnover in a local government department. *Mediterranean Journal of Social Sciences, 5*(2), 141–153.

Piven, F. F. (2006). *Challenging Authority — How Ordinary People Change America*. Lanham, MD: Rowman & Littlefield.

Potrafke, N. (2010). Does government ideology influence deregulation of product markets? Empirical evidence from OECD countries. *Public Choice, 143*(1), 135–155.

Powell, G. B., & Whitten, G. D. (1993). A cross-national analysis of economic voting: Taking account of the political context. *American Journal of Political Science, 37*(2), 391–414.

Radaelli, C. M. (1995). The role of knowledge in the policy process. *Journal of European Public Policy, 2*(2), 159–183.

Ragusa, J. M. (2010). The lifecycle of public policy: An event history analysis of repeals to landmark legislative enactments, 1951–2006. *American Politics Research, 38*(6), 1015–1051.

Rast, J. (2012). Why history (still) matters time and temporality in urban political analysis. *Urban Affairs Review, 48*(1), 3–36.

Rees, G. (1985). Regional restructuring, class change, and political action: Preliminary comments on the 1984–1985 miners' strike in South Wales. *Environment and Planning D: Society and Space, 3*(4), 389–406.

Rhoads, R. A., & Mina, L. (2001). The student strike at the National Autonomous University of Mexico: A political analysis. *Comparative Education Review, 45*(3), 334–353.

Rickne, J. (2013). Labor market conditions and social insurance in China. *China Economic Review, 27*(4), 52–68.

Rodrik, D., Subramanian, A., & Trebbi, F. (2004). Institutions rule: The primacy of institutions over geography and integration in economic development. *Journal of Economic Growth, 9*(2), 131–165.

Rohde, D. W., & Simon, D. M. (1985). Presidential vetoes and congressional response: A study of institutional conflict. *American Journal of Political Science, 29*(3), 397–427.

Rothenberg, L. S., & Sanders, M. S. (2000). Lame-duck politics: Impending departure and the votes on impeachment. *Political Research Quarterly, 53*(3), 523–536.

Rothstein, B. (2011). *The Quality of Government: Corruption, Social Trust, and Inequality in International Perspective.* Chicago: University of Chicago Press.

Roubini, N., Swagel, P. L., Alesina, A., & *et al.* (1996). Political stability and economic growth. *Journal of Economic Growth, 1*(2), 189–211.

Rubinson, R. (1977). Dependence, government revenue, and economic growth, 1955–1970. *Studies in Comparative International Development (SCID), 12*(2), 3–28.

Rucht, D., & Neidhardt, F. (2002). Towards a 'Movement Society'? On the possibilities of institutionalizing social movements. *Social Movement Studies, 1*(1), 7–30.

Rudolph, T. J., & Evans, J. (2005). Political trust, ideology, and public support for government spending. *American Journal of Political Science, 49*(3), 660–671.

Rueda, D. (2007). Social democracy constrained: Indirect taxation in industrialized democracies. *British Journal of Political Science, 37*(4), 619–641.

Sachs, J. D., & Warner, A. M. (1997). Sources of slow growth in African economies. *Journal of African Economies, 6*(3), 335–376.

Schattschneider, E. E. (1942). *Party Government: American Government in Action.* New York: Farrar and Rinehart.

Schmidt, M. G. (1996). When parties matter: A review of the possibilities and limits of partisan influence on public policy. *European Journal of Political Research, 30*(2), 155–183.

Schmidt, M. G., & Beyer, J. (1992). *Datensammlung zur parteipolitischen Zusammensetzung von Regierungen*, University of Heidelberg.

Schmidt-Sørensen, J. B. (1992). The profit share rate, wages and employment in collective bargaining. *European Journal of Political Economy, 8*(1), 105–113.

Schumacher, G. (2015). When does the left do the right thing? A study of party position change on welfare policies. *Party Politics, 21*(1), 68–79.

Shelton, C. A. (2007). The size and composition of government expenditure. *Journal of Public Economics, 91*(11–12), 2230–2260.

Shugart, M. S. (1995). The electoral cycle and institutional sources of divided presidential government. *American Political Science Review, 89*(2), 327–343.

Skocpol, T. (2000). *The Missing Middle: Working Families and the Future of American Social Policy.* New York: WW Norton & Company.

Starke, P. (2006). The politics of welfare state retrenchment: A literature review. *Social Policy & Administration, 40*(1), 104–120.

Stasavage, D. (2003). *Public Debt and the Birth of the Democratic State: France and Great Britain 1688–1789.* Cambridge: Cambridge University Press.

Steinberger, P. J. (1985). *Ideology and the Urban Crisis*. NY: State University of New York Press.

Strang, D., & Chang, P. M. Y. (1993). The International Labor Organization and the welfare state: Institutional effects on national welfare spending, 1960–80. *International Organization, 47*(2), 235–262.

Strøm, K. (1990). *Minority Government and Majority Rule*. Cambridge: Cambridge University Press.

Sundquist, J. L. (1988). Needed: A political theory for the new era of coalition government in the United States. *Political Science Quarterly, 103*(4), 613.

Sundquist, J. L. (1989). Can divided government be made to work? *Brookings Review, 7*(2), 14–15.

Tanzi, V., & Davoodi, H. (1998). *The Welfare State, Public Investment, and Growth*, pp. 41–60. Springer, Berlin.

Tarrow, S. G. (2011). *Power in Movement: Social Movements and Contentious Politics*. Cambridge: Cambridge University Press.

Taylorgooby, P. (2002). *Welfare States Under Pressure*. New York: Sage.

Thomas, S. (1994). *How Women Legislate*. Oxford: Oxford University Press.

Tilly, C., & Tarrow, S. (2006). *Contentious Politics*. Oxford: Oxford University Press.

Touraine, A. (1985). An introduction to the study of social movements. *Social Research, 52*(4), 749–787.

Treisman, D. (2015). Income, democracy, and leader turnover. *American Journal of Political Science, 59*(4), 927–942. doi: 10.1111/ajps.12135.

Treisman, D., & Gimpelson, V. (2001). Political business cycles and Russian elections, or the manipulations of 'Chudar'. *British Journal of Political Science, 31*(02), 225–246.

Tucker, B. A., & Russell, R. F. (2004). The influence of the transformational leader. *Journal of Leadership & Organizational Studies, 10*(4), 103–111.

Tufte, E. R. (1980). *Political Control of the Economy*. Princeton: Princeton University Press.

Van Kersbergen, K. (2003). *Social Capitalism: A Study of Christian Democracy and the Welfare State*. New York: Routledge.

Vanden, H. E. (2007). Social movements, hegemony, and new forms of resistance. *Latin American Perspectives: A Journal on Capitalism and Socialism, 34*(2), 17–30.

Vivekanandan, B., & Kurian, N. (2005). *Welfare States and the Future*. New York: Palgrave Macmillan.

Walder, A. G. (1991). Workers, managers and the state: The reform era and the political crisis of 1989. *The China Quarterly, 127*, 467–492.

Wang, G., Chen, X.-Y., Qiao, F.-L., Wu, Z., & Huang, N. E. (2010). On intrinsic mode function. *Advances in Adaptive Data Analysis, 2*(03), 277–293.

Wasserstrom, J. N. (1991). *Student Protests in Twentieth-Century China: The View from Shanghai*. Stanford: Stanford University Press.

Weakliem, D. (1993). Class consciousness and political change: Voting and political attitudes in the British working class, 1964 to 1970. *American Sociological Review, 58*(3), 382–397.

Williams, M. H. (2006). *The Impact of Radical Right-wing Parties in West European Democracies*. US: Palgrave Macmillan.

Woldendorp, J. J., Keman, H., & Budge, I. (2013). *Party Government in 48 Democracies (1945–1998): Composition — Duration — Personnel*. London: Springer Science & Business Media.

Wooldridge, J. M. (1995). Selection corrections for panel data models under conditional mean independence assumptions. *Journal of Econometrics, 68*(1), 115–132.

Wu, Z., & Huang, N. E. (2009). Ensemble empirical mode decomposition: A noise-assisted data analysis method. *Advances in Adaptive Data Analysis, 1*(01), 1–41.

Index

A

activity(-ies), 101, 112
administration, 26
administrative system, 2
agnostic, 32
alliances, 41
AMECO (annual macro-economic database of the European Commission), 107
American politics, 104
anticipation, 123
attention, 101
attenuation, 28

B

balance, 104
bankruptcy, 80
bargaining, 6, 123
bicameralism, 2
bidirectional, 101
binary, 112
Bureau, 100
bureaucracy, 50

C

cabinet, 1, 36
candidate, 100
capitalist, 103
challenges, 78
civil servant, 31
cleavage, 78
coalition, 123
coalition cabinet, 3
coefficients, 111
cold war, 81
communication, 49
Comparative Political Data Set, 34
comparisons, 97
composition, 49
conflict, 50
Congress, 2
Congressional seats, 4
consideration, 109
constant, 109
contradictory, 79, 83
convergence, 112
correlation coefficient, 107

Cosine, 9
Cosine distance, 1, 9
Cosine distance method, 10
cost, 101
credibility, 30
criteria, 112
cultures, 122
curve, 114

D

data, 7
dataset, 34
definition, 109
degree, 10, 110
delivery, 30
demarcation, 79
democracy(-ies), 27, 98
demographic characteristic, 31
dependence, 91
development, v
diagram, 14
dissolution, 35
distribution, 118
divided government, 2
division, 8
dummy, 109
dynamics, 82

E

economic data series, 49
economic fluctuation, 25
economic growth, vi, 25
economy, v
education, 34
efficiency, 30
election, 26, 35, 99
election campaigns, 80
ensemble empirical mode decomposition, 25
enthusiasm, 104
environment, 103
equations, 101
error term, 101
estimation, 117
Euclidean distance, 1, 9
Europe, 3, 104
evaluation, 112
exaggeration, 80
executive, 1
expenditure, 90

F

feminist, 122
financial crises, 103
fixed effects model, 77, 91
fluctuations, vi, 49
formal model, 29
formulation, 30
France, 3
freedom, 110
frequency, 49
function, 8, 109

G

GDP, 18
gender, 100
globalization, 79
government, 2
government effectiveness, vi
government revenue, 18, 111
government turnover, 25, 28
growth, 114

H

hegemony, 36
hereditary, 26
heterogeneity, 109

heteroscedasticity, 91
history, 80
hypothesis, 106

I

identification, 97
ideological conflicts, 80
ideological division, v
ideological turnover, 110
ideology(-ies), 7, 24
impact, 101
implementation, 30
impulse, 112
income, 123
incumbency, 77
incumbent, 29
independence, 13
independent variable, 41
indicators, 8
industrialized countries, 25
industry, 81
inflation, 29
inflation rate, 121
influence, 50, 111
informal institutions, 27
information, 34
instability, 31
integration, 80
intervals, 112
investigation, 123
investment, 30, 33

K

knowledge, 101

L

labor, 4
lagged effect, 99
lagged regressors, 111
Lagrange Multiplier, 90
lame-duck, 29
large-N, 97
leadership, 5, 25
left-wing, vi
legislative branches, 1
legislature, 2
limitation, 123
local government, 30
long-term, vi

M

maximum, 36
measurement, 50
measurement methods, 1
mechanism, 114
memory, 104
methodology, 18
microeconomic, 28
minority government, 3
model, 111
modification, 81
motivation, 101
multi-power politics, 2

N

non-majority government, 3
North America, 104
null hypothesis, 112

O

occupy wall street movement, 99
OECD, 105
one-period, 20
ordinary least square, 90
orthogonality, 111
outcome, 27, 41

P

panel data, 27, 34
panel vector auto-regression model, 99
parameters, 111
parliament, 1
parliamentary, 35
participation rate, 87
parties-matter theory, 79
partisan politics, 78
partisanship, 29
party government, 1
party polarization, v
Pearson Correlation Coefficient, 10
penetration, 18
percentage, 7, 107
perception, 96
performance, 5
period, 110, 121
phenomenon, 29
policy, 14, 30
policy changes, 105
policy preferences, 105, 111
political business cycles, 29
political efficiency, 1
political pressures, 13, 30
population, 34
portfolios, 6
position, 77
positive effect, 25
power, 104
predecessors, 26
premier, 3
president, 106
prime minister, 3
processes, 122
production, 123
productivity, 6, 30
proportion, 50, 81
proportional, 78
protection, 122
public policy, 79

Q

quality, 14, 81
Quality of Government, 34
quantitative analyses, 23

R

random effects model, 90
realms, 29
receipts, 111
recession, 110
reconstruction, 80
regression model, 18
reliability, 117
renovation, 80
Republican candidate, 100
research subjects, 98
reshuffle, 26
resignation, 35
retrenchment, 79
revolutions, 77
right-wing incumbency, vi
robustness, 20, 93, 117
roles, 29

S

sample, 93
sample size, 42
Schattschneider, 1
scholarship, 104
security, 27
shape, 98

shock, 116
short-term, vi
significance, 112
single party, 2
social security, 77
social security expenditure, 77
social welfare redistribution, 111
society, v
spillover effect, 78
standard deviations, 36
state, 3
stationary, 112
statistics, 100
strike index, 107
strikes, 99
structural break points, 25, 27
subtraction, 8
subversion, 103
succession, 26, 104
synthetic, 111
system, 3, 101

T

time-series data, 34
transitions, 103
transmission, 114
turnover, 26

U

unemployment, 82, 110
unemployment rate, 121
unified government, 2
union, 123
United States, 2
urbanization, 34

V

validity, 77
value, 49
variable, 10, 101
variation, 49
vectors, 9
visualization, 91

W

welfare, 82
West European, 78
work, 27
worker, 30, 104
World Bank, 34
World Governance Indicator, 34
World War II, 3
Worldwide Governance Indicators, 26

CPSIA information can be obtained
at www.ICGtesting.com
Printed in the USA
LVHW080814281218
601106LV00006B/10/P